J. M. Hart, Bernhard Ten Brink

A Syllabus of Anglo-Saxon Literature

J. M. Hart, Bernhard Ten Brink

A Syllabus of Anglo-Saxon Literature

ISBN/EAN: 9783337258825

Printed in Europe, USA, Canada, Australia, Japan

Cover: Foto ©ninafisch / pixelio.de

More available books at **www.hansebooks.com**

A

SYLLABUS

OF

ANGLO-SAXON LITERATURE

BY

J. M. HART

(UNIVERSITY OF CINCINNATI)

————

ADAPTED FROM BERNHARD TEN BRINK'S
GESCHICHTE DER ENGLISCHEN LITTERATUR

————

CINCINNATI
ROBERT CLARKE & CO
1881

ANGLO-SAXON LITERATURE.

CHAPTER I.

ROMAN BRITAIN.

1. The earliest known inhabitants of England belonged to the Keltic race, and were called Britons. When Julius Cæsar invaded the island, 55 B. C., they were still in a barbarous or semi-barbarous state. A serious attempt to annex the island permanently to the Roman empire was not made until 43 A. D., in the reign of Claudius. The work of conquest was continued during the reigns of Vespasian, Titus, and Domitian, and was complete by 85 A. D. From that time until the 5th century Britannia and the southern part of Scotia were administered as a Roman province. Roman law, manners, and letters were introduced. Large towns grew up, *e.g.*, York, London, Lincoln. There was a thriving trade between the island and the continent. Extensive remains of roads, aqueducts, tesselated pavements, and the like, still bear witness to the thoroughness of the conquest. When the Roman world became christianized, Britain also shared in the conversion. By the middle of the 4th century the island had its hierarchy and a well developed system of religious orders and monasteries.

We do not know whether the primitive Britons possessed anything that could be called a literature of their own, and, if so, of what character. Roman literature was imported, so to speak, but we have no means of ascertaining whether it exerted any strong direct influence on the mass of the natives. Britain was for the Romans nothing more than a military outpost. The garrison consisted usually of 20,000—30,000 men, stationed at important strategic points, which were connected by military roads. The children of the leading native families were probably educated at first in the city of Rome, as hostages, subsequently at home in Roman schools under the supervision of the Roman governor. The inferior population in and around the Roman towns and camps acquired from soldiers and public officials a knowledge of the Latin tongue sufficient for the ordinary intercourse of life. But the rural population, which must have largely predominated, remained in all probability Keltic in habits, tastes, feelings, and speech. Roman administration, it is true, was as energetic and efficient in Britain as elsewhere. It suppressed, for instance, the savage rites and practices of Druidism, and secured to every man protection in the enjoyment of life and property. But we have no warrant for believing that Roman culture *pervaded* and transformed Britain as it pervaded Gaul and Spain. It was at best only an exotic, and it was swept away by the first breath of adversity.

2. In consequence of the dangers which threatened the continental and more vital parts of the empire, the Roman army was withdrawn from the island early in the 5th century, and the Britons were left to struggle unaided against their Keltic kinsmen, the Picts and Scots on the north, and the Irish on the west (the coast of Wales), and against the German tribes that came in ever-growing numbers from across the North Sea. Tradition tells us that these Germans were invited by the Britons to help them against the Picts and Scots; after defeating the northern invaders in a series of bloody battles, the Germans then turned their arms against

their hosts, the Britons. The tradition is to be found in
Bede, Nennius, and Geoffrey of Monmouth; the story
of Hengist and Horsa, Vortigern and Rowena, as it has
been graphically narrated by Geoffrey, is doubtless familiar to most readers. But it is impossible at the present day to unravel the true and the fabulous in the
story. There is evidence going to show that Germanic
tribes had settled in considerable numbers along the
eastern and south-eastern coast, even before the end of
the 4th century. The only fact which need concern the
student of literature is that German-speaking tribes began a conquest of the island in the course of the 5th
century, and had finished it substantially by the end of
the 6th century. This second conquest was in every respect unlike the first. It was not a mere military occu-
pation, it was a settlement in mass. The invaders
brought with them or sent for their families, and sought
to make the land their lasting home. Hence the war between them and the Britons could result only in the
total subjection and dispossession of the weaker party.
The Britons were finally dispossessed. Many were slain
outright in battle, others killed off in petty feuds, others
driven across the channel to the Armorican peninsula in
France, still others hemmed in among the mountain
fastnesses of Wales. By the year 610 the eastern part
of the island as far north as the Firth of Forth, all the
southern and central parts, and the western part (except
Wales, Cornwall, and Devonshire) as far north as the
river Mersey, were in the hands of the Germans. It is
usually asserted that the war against the Britons was one
of utter extermination. But it is more probable that
numerous small isolated communities of Britons sur-
vived in the western and south-western portions of what
is now England proper, and were only absorbed in the
course of centuries, by the slow process of intermarriage.

Henceforth the country is called by its German name of England.

3. The permanent vestiges of the British race in the land that was once their own may be briefly summed up as follows. The Kelto-British tongue has disappeared wholly from England proper, and survives only in Welsh, now spoken by about a million of people. A dialectic variety known as Cornish became extinct early in the present century. According to some scholars, certain peculiarities in the pronunciation of the rural population in the south-western and western counties of England are of Keltic origin. The Britons, in disappearing, transmitted to their conquerors a few Latin words imposed upon them by the Romans, *e.g.*, *castrum*, in early English *ceaster*, in modern English *caster*, *chester*, *cester*, as in the name Chester, and in the compounds Dorchester, Winchester, Lancaster, Leicester, and the like. Also *colonia*, in Lincoln; *strata*, in our word 'street;' *porta*, in Newport; *milia* in 'mile.' Probably also our words 'tile' and 'pear' were derived from the Romans through the Britons. Concerning other words of Latin origin, *e.g.*, 'candel,' 'bishop,' 'priest,' 'mass,' it is impossible to decide whether they were transmitted through the Britons, or were borrowed by the English directly from Rome. Furthermore, the early English adopted and retained some Keltic words. These are not numerous. They are chiefly names of familiar household objects, or names of places, especially rivers. Among the latter are Thames, Trent, Tweed, Severn, Avon (which is Keltic for running water in general), and the group of names Usk, Ux, Wis (in Wisbec), Eske, Ouse—all modifications of the Keltic *uisc* 'water,' which is also found in the Highland *usquebagh*, corrupted into 'whisky,' and standing for a primitive *uisce vaha*, meaning 'water of life;' but this word *usquebagh* has been introduced into English in quite recent times. To the former class belong the words 'basket,' 'bran,' 'wicket,' 'clout,' 'crag.' An American will readily understand the fate of the Keltic language in England, by comparing it with that of the Indian language in this country. Although the Indians themselves have disappeared from the greater part of the United States, their language survives in Susquehanna, Juniata, Potomac, Mississippi, Ohio, Niagara, etc., and in wigwam, wampum, squaw, tomahawk, moccasin, succotash, etc.

There are no traces of any influence exerted by the Britons upon early English literature. The invaders brought with them not only their own language, but also their own—still heathen—worship, and the germs and even the beginning of a distinctively German poetic literature. So long as the contest lasted, and for centuries afterward, literature in England was either distinctly German, or was based upon the general Roman Catholic literature of the continent. It is not until the 12th century, after England had been conquered by the Normans, that we observe a sudden and curious outgrowth of British, *i.e.*, Welsh literature. But this point can be treated only in connection with the Arthurian cycle of romance.

CHAPTER II.

THE GERMAN CONQUERORS.

4. The Germans who settled in England came from Jutland, Schleswig, and Holstein, and from the coast to the west of the Elbe, known as Friesland. They were a sturdy, warlike race, inured from childhood to privation and danger. Their home was preëminently a training-

school for sailors. They and their successors, the Danes and Norsemen, were as sea-robbers the terror of Europe. The 5th century was a turning point in history; it marked the prostration of the Western Roman empire. Northern Gaul was seized by the Franks, Southern Gaul by the Goths, Eastern Gaul by the Burgundians. The Langobards established themselves even in Northern Italy. The Christian church itself, which had inspired the noblest hopes and efforts of humanity, appeared in danger of an eclipse. Culture and knowledge were scarcely safe in the refuge of the cloister. Everywhere was to be seen the foot-print of a ruthless heathen invader. No wonder, then, that the Latin writers (chiefly ecclesiastics) of the 5th and 6th centuries indulged in bitter lamentations. The Frank and the Saxon, the Goth and the Dane, were in their sight devils sent by an angry God to punish the world for sin. Their sufferings were too recent, their imaginations too heated, for them to think clearly. Yet it is from them that we derive our knowledge of the great Germanic Migration. The Germans themselves were too busy fighting and plundering to think of recording their deeds autobiographically, even had they possessed the literary ability. It is necessary, therefore, to receive with caution the statements of Latin writers concerning the character of the German conquerors. That these latter were fierce in battle and eager for booty, is unquestionable. They were furthermore given to immoderate eating and drinking, and their seasons of warlike exertion were followed by long spells of idle revelry. But they can not possibly have been the monsters or savages that we read of in early chronicles or even in some modern histories. In comparison with modern civilized man, they were quick to shed blood; but by the side of the Romans of the Republic, they appear almost humane. We may well doubt if the so-called barbarian Germans during the whole period of the

5th and 6th centuries inflicted in all Europe as much misery as was wrought by Julius Cæsar alone in the eight years that he was engaged in subduing Gaul.

We can trace the movements and study the features of the German migration on the continent with tolerable accuracy. The records, although sparse and vitiated by prejudice, are in the main intelligible. But the conquest of England is hopelessly obscure. We do not possess a single contemporary record, nor indeed any record that is self-consistent or even plausible. All that we can do is to note here and there a point in the light afforded by the study of general European history.

The invaders of England were all of the same race, yet there was diversity enough among them to lead us to establish a threefold grouping into the Jutes (from Jutland), the Angles (from Schleswig–Holstein), and the Saxons, an offshoot of the great family of that name then occupying the regions along the middle and lower Elbe. The Jutes are said to have seized upon Kent; the Angles occupied the eastern, the Saxons the western and southern parts of the island. All three groups spoke the same language, but in forms that differed enough to be called dialects. These main dialects subsist to the present day, and are called the northern, the southern, and the Kentish. Each has its sub-varieties. In general we may say that at no time in the history of England have the inhabitants of one county had much difficulty in understanding the inhabitants of any other. There has never been such a dividing line between north and south as exists for instance in continental Germany between High German and Low. The fitting title to be given to the common speech of England in these early days before the Norman Conquest is a question which has been much discussed of late. One set of scholars, including Mr. Sweet, Mr. Freeman, Mr. Morris, Prof. ten Brink, assert that the only rightful title is ' Old-English.' Another and more numerous set prefer to call it, for the sake of exactness, 'Anglo-Saxon,' reserving the term 'Old-English' for the period after the Norman Conquest. Each terminology has its advantages and its disadvantages. In the following pages 'Anglo-Saxon' will be employed wherever it seems desirable.

5. Anglo-Saxon was an offshoot of Low, *i.e.* North-German speech, and resembled very closely the so-called Old-Saxon, the language which was spoken between the Lower Rhine and the Elbe and of which we possess considerable literary remains of the 9th century. Anglo-Saxon and Old-Saxon, in fact, resemble each other so closely that an English monk of those days, removing from Winchester to Paderborn, must have been able to make himself at home almost immediately. As a matter of history we know that many English monks did emigrate to this Rhine–Elbe region in the 8th and 9th centuries, to labor as missionaries, and that they exerted a perceptible influence in shaping the ecclesiastical prose form of Old-Saxon. One single fact will be enough to illustrate the kinship of the two languages. The Anglo-Saxon poem on the creation and fall of man, commonly called *Genesis* and once attributed to Caedmon, was published by Franciscus Junius in 1655. Until 1875 it was supposed, as a matter of course, to be perfectly pure Anglo-Saxon. But in 1875 Professor Sievers showed conclusively that about one fifth of the poem is interpolated, and that this interpolation is a fragment of an Anglo-Saxon version of an earlier Old-Saxon poem on the same subject. Whoever converted the Old-Saxon poem into Anglo-Saxon suffered inadvertently a few words and phrases to remain, that are peculiar to Old-Saxon and are not found elsewhere in English literature. Yet the general resemblance of the two languages is so great that these un-English elements escaped the notice

of scholars and editors for upwards of two centuries. See § 21.

A few remarks upon the more general features of Anglo-Saxon speech will not be out of place. It is rich in words for weapons, such as the sword, the shield, the spear, in words descriptive of combat, and in words relating to ships and the sea. It impresses us immediately as the speech of a fighting, sea-faring folk. On the other hand it is rich in words expressive of moods and emotions of the mind. We have lost many of these latter terms, having substituted for them words of Norman-French or Latin or Greek origin. Those which remain represent the subtler and more mysterious side of our nature. There is one feature of Anglo-Saxon which does not seem to have attracted the notice of scholars in England, although German scholars have laid much stress on it. Namely, its tendency toward introspection, and the favoring of a sad or at least plaintive disposition. This trait, it may be remarked in passing, still subsists in our modern speech. With all its robustness, its common-sense power of adapting itself to the realities of the world, English, contrasted with the Romance languages and with continental German, still moves with an undercurrent of sadness. See § 18.

6. Our knowledge of the institutions and the religion of the Angles and Saxons at the time of their settlement has been obtained almost altogether from a study of kindred relations on the continent. The people were divided into three classes : the nobles, *corlas;* the simple freemen, *ceorlas;* and the slaves. The chief among the nobles, the princes, gathered around them a retinue of devoted personal adherents, the *thegnas,* or ' thanes.' As the princes grew in power and dignity, and—by reason of greater familiarity with Roman institutions—assumed more and more of the prerogatives of the Roman emperors, these *thegnas* attained to the position of a *court-nobility*, outranking the elder hereditary nobility of the *eorlas*. They were enriched by gifts of land conquered in war, and held their possessions upon condition of rendering military service. We thus find the outlines of the feudal system clearly marked in England in the Anglo-Saxon period, although the system reached its full development only after and in consequence of the Norman Conquest. This feudal or semi-feudal spirit is worthy of especial note, for it pervades all the early poetry of England. In the poetry of heathen origin it is of course conspicuous. The prince is constantly described as the giver of rings and gold bracelets, of costly helmets and trusty swords. A right-minded prince is a free giver; an ignoble prince is grasping and miserly. On the other hand, a loyal thane is one who shows himself worthy of his lord's munificence, standing by him in danger and perishing with him in battle. This notion of giving and receiving, of generosity and personal attachment, is the key-note of all early German heroic poetry. In Anglo-Saxon literature we find it almost as pronounced in Christian as in heathen poetry. God is the giver of life and health; life is a *loan* from the Maker, and death a *calling-in* of the loan. Christ is the prince of glory, and the apostles are his faithful thanes. Satan and his companions are faithless thanes, and their rebellion is an ungrateful breach of allegiance.

7. We know even less of the religion of the Angles and Saxons than of their political institutions. Several quite recent discoveries have shaken the confidence of scholars in former theories based upon the *Edda*. It is at best doubtful whether the subject of Old-German heathen belief can be made intelligible to any one not familiar with the general processes and results of comparative mythology. Only a few of the striking features will be given here, and even these will be of a negative rather than of a positive character. The Angles and Saxons, like their continental kinsmen, worshipped certain so-called divinities, Othin, Thor, Loki, Freya, &c. These divinities were originally nature-myths, that is, forces or phenomena of nature, such as the wind, thunder, fire, the fertility of the earth, personified and invested with human attributes, male or female. There is an unquestionable similarity, or parallelism, between the German divinities, and those of Greece and of India, so much so that scholars are agreed in assigning all three groups to one common primitive Indo-European conception of nature. The differences among the three are due in general to the greater or less thoroughness with which a nature-force or phenomenon has been reduced to purely human shape and proportions, or—to use the technical term—has been *anthropomorphized*. In this respect the German group stands midway between the Indian and the Greek. The Vedic divinities, *e.g.* Agni, the god of fire, Vâya, the god of the wind, Indra, the god of the clear sky, Usha, the goddess of the dawn, are still unmistakable natureforces; they can scarcely be called 'persons' at all. On the other hand Jupiter, Neptune, Apollo, Venus, &c., have lost almost every trace of their origin and have become mere men and women of extraordinary powers. Whereas the German Othin, Thor and their associates, . although no longer mere myths, are not yet mere men and women. · They lack that sharpness of outline and that perfect intelligibility which constitute the charm of the Olympic gods in Homer. They come down and move among men, they fight side by side with heroes, but they never cease to be misty, supernatural, phantasmagoric.

We know far less of the Germanic system than of the Greek or the Indian, and the explanation is obvious enough. Both Greeks and Hindoos developed their systems naturally and fully, not only in literature but in painting and sculpture, before coming in contact with Christianity. The Germans, on the contrary, were converted to Christianity before they had fairly begun the literary or pictorial expression of their heathen conception. In accepting Christian doctrines they gave up deliberately their early beliefs. It became a matter of conscience with them to ignore everything anterior to Christianity as crude and barbarous. The priests of the Roman Catholic church were inflexible in their efforts to eradicate whatever savored of heathenism in manners, customs, and even speech. There is more than one passage in the poem of Beowulf, for instance, which has evidently been altered to suit ecclesiastical requirements. It is not surprising, then, that the remains we possess of early heathen literature should be so fragmentary and confused. The wonder is rather that so much should have escaped the general destruction.

Concerning the religion of the heathen Germans, we should not be safe in asserting more than the following : it had no priesthood, no distinct order to mediate between men and gods ; it exacted no sacrifice of human blood, although victims, usually captives, were occasionally slain upon the altar ; it paid great respect to women, investing them with a quasi-prophetic sacred character ; it looked upon cowardice and treachery as the basest of vices ; it held out the hope of a future life reproducing the main features of life on earth ; its service consisted chiefly of warlike hymns or chants.

•

CHAPTER III.

GENERAL FEATURES OF THE EARLY POETRY.

8. The earliest poetry among the Germans was of a religious kind, in the shape of hymns to the gods upon solemn occasions. Being addressed directly to the gods, it was necessarily an expression of mythological conceptions. And as the hymns were sung, or at least chanted, they were composed in short strophes or stanzas. Remains of such hymnic poetry are quite evident in the Edda. In Anglo-Saxon literature they are barely discernible.

In Germany proper and in England hymnic poetry was superseded by heroic verse. To understand the growth of this latter system, we must keep in view the general tendencies of European history. The fifth century was a turning-point not only for the Roman world but for the German conquerors themselves. It was the beginning of their 'heroic age.' To us, who study the events of the great Migration in a critical spirit, with the aid of contemporary Latin records, such leaders as Theoderic, King of the Goths, are actual men like ourselves, without a trace of the supernatural. But it was quite otherwise with the illiterate but imaginative descendants of the Goths, the Franks, or the Burgundians, in the 6th and subsequent centuries. Popular imagination, stimulated by oral tradition, endowed the great chieftains of the 5th century with superhuman strength and courage, and crowned their deeds with the halo of romance. Great men became, in a word, 'heroes,' and their deeds became the theme of popular poetry. This secular poetry, in supplanting the elder hymns, retained not a few of their mythological elements. Attributes and actions of the gods were transferred to the heroes, thereby making them semi-mythical. The process will be treated more fully in the remarks upon the Beowulf poem, § 12. For the present it will be enough to say that the new heroic poetry first found expression in short pieces, commemorating a single exploit of some well known hero. The poem places us, without any prelude, in the very midst of the action, and the actors reveal their character and antecedents by what they do and say. A striking instance is the *Hildebrands-lied*, in Old-German of the 8th century. It begins : " I heard tell that Hildebrand and Hadubrand, in between the two armies, made ready their armor, girded on their swords. And Hildebrand, he was the elder, inquired of the other, in few words, who his father might be, &c." He himself is the father; he had fled from home twenty years before, on account of political troubles, and had taken refuge with Dietrich (*i.e.*, Theoderic), at the court of Attila, King of the Huns. Now he is returning home at the head of an army, to recover his possessions, but is stopped by his son, who has in the meanwhile grown to manhood. By dint of questioning, the father finds out that his foe is his son, and declares himself. But the son refuses to believe, reviles him for 'an old Hun,' and insists upon fighting. The father's lament at being thus forced to an unnatural combat is extremely touching. The poem breaks off at the first encounter, so that what we have is only a fragment. Most scholars are of the opinion that it ended tragically, with the death of the son.

The strophe or stanza of the elder hymnic poetry was unsuited to these new heroic poems, which were not sung but recited. It was therefore discarded, except in the literature of Scandinavia, and for it was substituted a continuous flow of verse. The difference between stanza-verse and continuous verse may be readily felt by comparing the *Faery Queen* with *Paradise Lost.* In a

narrative piece of any length, it is impossible for the
poet to express each successive thought or action in a
fixed number of lines. Either he will have too little to
say, and consequently will eke out the stanza with a
superfluous line or two; or he will have too much to say,
and will carry over the sentence into the succeeding
stanza, thereby occasioning an awkward *enjambement*, or
'straddling.'

In the course of time the short episodic poems grouped
themselves into longer poems, commemorating a series
of deeds by a certain hero, or the fortunes of a hero and
his companions, or a long chain of events in which
many members of a family or leaders of a tribe partici-
pated. Such longer pieces may be called 'epics.' An
instance of a modern poem in imitation of a medieval
epic is Tennyson's *Enid*; on the other hand the *Lady of
Shalott*, like the *Hildebrands-lied*, is episodic. The *Iliad*
and the *Odyssey* are examples of epic poetry in its perfec-
tion. Finally, all the poems, episodic and epic, and all
the scattered traditions relating to one set of heroes and
events constitute what is called a 'cycle' of fable.
Thus, Tennyson's *Lady of Shalott*, *Sir Galahad*, *Idylls of
the King*, &c., are parts of the great medieval cycle of
King Arthur and the Knights of the Round Table.

9. There was not among the early Germans a separate class of singers or poets. All, from the King down
to the simple *ceorl*, had the right to sing in public assem-
blies. It was even expected of every one present at the
board, when the mead-cup and the harp were passed
around, that he should contribute his share to the evening's entertainment. The custom, which still lingers in
the *Rundgesang* of modern Germany, is well illustrated
by the story told of Caedmon, see § 20. These old German and English 'songs' were not songs in the modern
sense; they were 'recitals' of the great deeds of popu-

lar heroes. Both speaker and listener were familiar, through long practice, with the leading events in the history of the tribe or the nation, and with the ancestry, life, character, and habits of each hero. Hence the abruptness of such poetry. The singer has a right to take for granted that his hearers are as familiar as himself with the substance of the story he is to narrate. He not only plunges boldly *in medias res, e.g.*, in the *Hildebrands-lied* above mentioned, but he interrupts the course of the main narrative with allusions to persons and events indirectly connected with it. Such allusions are often quite brief. They can not in strictness be called obscure, for doubtless they were understood at once by the original hearers. But to a modern reader they are extremely difficult.

The substance of the stories handed down to us in Anglo-Saxon and other Old-German is eminently a product of the popular mind. Generation after generation labored upon the stories before they assumed the shape in which we have them. No less popular is the form of verse. It is at once simple, powerful, and flexible. It was not too difficult for the common man to use, yet in the mouth of an accomplished narrator it was capable of expressing all that the mind of those early days was capable of conceiving.

This Old-German verse is usually called, after its most striking feature, 'alliterative.' The number of syllables in the verse is not fixed exactly; nor can we say that the verse is divided into 'feet.' There is no terminal rime. Each full verse (line), as printed in recent editions, is to be read in two sections nearly but not quite equal. In early editions the sections were printed as separate lines. The two sections produce an effect not unlike that of a modern 'couplet,' for they are coupled together by certain words beginning with the same sound, *i.e.*, they are said to 'alliterate.' Thus:

flota fâmighals   fugle gelicost
the ship foamy-necked, to a fowl most like

The three *f*-sounds alliterate. Any vowel may alliterate with any other vowel, *e.g.*

Thâ côm in gân   ealdor thegna
Then came in-going the prince of the thanes

The verb *côm* with the dependent compound infinitive
in-gân is equivalent to the modern ' entered.' The *i* of
the prefix *in* alliterates with the *ea* of *ealdor*. Strictly a
consonant can alliterate only with itself; but there are
some licenses. In the most correct verse there are two
alliterative sounds in the first section of the line and one
in the second. But very frequently there is only one in
each, and sometimes we find two in each, although not
often in Anglo-Saxon poetry. It has been stated above
that there is no terminal rime in alliterative verse. This
is strictly true of the heathen poetry, and also in general
of the Christian poetry until a comparatively late period,
when we find rimes creeping in. They are an imitation
of the Latin hymns of the Catholic church, and the
forerunners of our modern system. Hence they are
nearly always to be considered as symptoms of a decline
of the early alliterative system. See § 30.

The alliteration rests usually on the emphatic words
of the sentence. Sound and sense, therefore, go hand
in hand and help each other: When properly read, an
alliterative poem is easy, flowing, and dignified. It
has moreover a peculiar power which the scholar alone
will appreciate and which can not be reproduced in any
modern imitation. One reason is that our early speech
abounded in standing epithets, and set phrases and form-
ulae, which have ceased to exist. Besides, modern imi-
tators fail to perceive that alliteration is something more
than the mere recurrence of a certain sound two or three
times in the course of the line. The line itself has a

structure of its own; it is, as already stated, a couplet in which the first part is balanced by the second. We need only compare a line from the Beowulf-poem with a line from Tennyson.

The Anglo-Saxon poet says:

> Gewât thâ ofer wâegholm winde gefŷsed
> Flota fâmighals fugle gelîcost
> Went then over the wave-top, by the wind urged,
> The ship &c.

The *ge* in *gewât* is unaccented and the following *w* alliterates with those in *wdeg* and *winde*. The whole line makes upon the ear a very different effect from Tennyson's:

> They wept and wailed but led the way

Tennyson also gives us, it is true, three *w*'s, but we feel that the phrase ' but led the way' does not 'balance' the preceding, and we wait instinctively for the next line:

> To where a little shallop lay

to complete the effect, by means of its rime 'way : lay.' But this rime is no alliteration.

10. Anglo-Saxon poetry differs from modern English in its style also. The language is synthetic, *i.e.*, it denotes grammatical relations by varying the forms of words. It is not tied down to the modern logical order: subject, copula, predicate. The poet is, in general, free to arrange the words with a view to their effect upon the ear and the imagination. Hence inversions are quite common. There is also a marked tendency to amplification. An object is described, an action narrated by successive sets of phrases, that are not to be taken as repetitions but as shiftings of the view-point. Thus, in the passage cited, § 9, the ship is spoken of as 'the floating thing,' then as 'the twining or curved stem.' The approach to land is given in three phrases; they (the mari-

ners) saw 'the strand-cliffs,' 'the steep hills,' 'the broad
sea-promontories.' In modern speech such amplification
might be wearisome; but in primitive poetry it adds life
and variety. The poet seems to be reproducing from
memory his impressions in the order in which they were
made upon his mind. Finally, the language is rich in
plain and obvious similies, but not in formal comparisons.
The body is called *bán-loca*, the 'bone-case;' to make a
speech is 'to unlock the treasure of words in one's breast.'
The scream of the ravens gathering around the corpses
after the fight is called the 'evening-song;' the hissing
of the sword in battle is also a 'song.' The battle itself
is called *ecga gelác*, the 'play of edges.'

It was stated, § 9 beginning, that there was no separate class of poets. Song-craft was the common posses-
sion of all. Nevertheless certain men must have been
more richly endowed than others with poetic gifts. They
were sweet singers by eminence. Some few excepted,
they have not left a record of their names, nor can we
identify their names with any of the poems that we
possess. But the tradition of such poets was preserved
until late in the Middle Ages. A notable instance is
Horant, who figures in the great German epic of *Gudrun*,
and of whom the poem tells us that when he sang, the
birds ceased to warble, the sick forgot their pains, the
workman stopped, the beasts of the wood, the fish in the
water, the very insects in the grass, paused to listen.
Horant, then, is the counterpart to Orpheus. Both name
and works of at least one poet among the Angles and
Saxons, namely Cynewulf, have been preserved. See § 24.

In estimating our early heathen poetry, we should
never forget that we have only disjointed remnants of
what was once a large body of literature. Had we all
the popular narrative poems current in England in the
7th, 8th, and 9th centuries, our knowledge would be en-
hanced a hundred-fold. We must also learn to discrim-

inate carefully between the part played by the folk at
large and that played by the individual in the composition
of such poetry. The substance of the poem, *i.e.*, the
story, the heroes, their character and exploits, were the
common tradition of the people. In these respects there '
was no room for poetic 'invention' in our modern
sense. Whoever in Old England undertook to tell in
verse of the deeds of the forefathers was not at liberty to
add or to change a name, an incident, or a trait of character. All that he could call his own was the *manner of
telling*. And, as Lowell has put it:—

> He tells it last, who tells it best.

We can imagine a favorite story passed along from generation to generation, until some one poet arises, who
succeeds in telling it so well that his version becomes the
final one. Henceforth all that remains to be done is to
preserve it in this shape. The name of the poet may
disappear utterly; the story itself never was his; but the
version is his, even although it bear no name.

11. One more general feature of our early poetry
must be introduced in this place, although it obliges us
to anticipate somewhat the course of political events. It
was stated, § 4, that three varieties of speech, called dia-
alects, were spoken in England, viz., the northern (Northumbrian), the southern (West-Saxon, or Wessex), and
the Kentish. We learn from history that Northumbria
first rose to eminence in ecclesiastical, political, and literary matters. It took the lead throughout the 7th and
8th centuries. Most of the conspicuous men of England
prior to the 9th century were Northumbrians by birth or
by residence and education. Thus Bede, Caedmon,
Cynewulf, &c. It is highly probable, also, that the poem
of Beowulf was composed in Northumbria. We should
expect, therefore, to find the earliest literary remains

written in the Northumbrian dialect. But this is not the case. All the early poetry, heathen as well as Christian, and almost all the early prose, are in the Wessex dialect.

The only specimen of verse in the Northumbrian dialect of this period is a fragment of nine lines at the end of a Latin manuscript of Bede's *Historia*, see § 19, 20. If the earliest literature in England was composed in Northumbria, how can we account for the phenomenon that it has all been transmitted to us in the speech of Wessex? The explanation usually given is this. From the beginning of the 9th century Northumbria was ravaged more and more by the Danes. At one time it was completely in their power. Being heathens, they acted as the Angles and Saxons themselves had acted three centuries before. They plundered the monasteries, which were the seats of learning and the libraries of those days, and scattered or destroyed the manuscripts. Even Wessex was in danger, and was saved only through the genius and energy of King Alfred. It is commonly believed by scholars that in or before the reign of King Alfred a great part of early Northumbrian poetry was transcribed and recast in Wessex forms, and that these Wessex versions have been handed down to us, while the Northumbrian originals perished. In consequence of the Danish invasions, the centre of political and literary activity was shifted from Northumbria to Wessex. The capital of King Alfred and his successors, Winchester, became the seat of learning. And it was here, in and around Winchester, that the first English prose literature originated. As will be shown in a subsequent place, King Alfred himself labored indefatigably in shaping this prose. Comparing the two great divisions of the island, then, we may say that Northumbria is entitled to the credit of creating our earliest poetry, Wessex to the two-fold credit of preserving that poetry and of creating our earliest prose.

CHAPTER IV.

BEOWULF AND OTHER HEATHEN POETRY.

12. The poem of Beowulf is by far the most important and interesting monument of early German poetry, not only by virtue of its length and the variety of incident it affords, but by its vigor of style and the light it throws upon manners and customs. The substance of the story is a blending of myth and history, and aptly illustrates what was stated § 8.

The germ of the story is mythical. Before the conquerors of England left their continental home, there had sprung up among them the myth of a divine being, Beowa, who overcomes a sea-monster, Grendel, and then a fire-dragon ; in the latter encounter he loses his own life. This Beowa is only another form of Frea, the god of warmth and fertility, and his death symbolizes the disappearance of summer at the approach of winter. The Germans brought the myth with them to Britain, and the names of Beowa and Grendel became attached to certain hills and lakes, *e.g.*, Beowanham, Grendlesmere. Around this mythical germ, or kernel, clustered subsequently the following historical incidents.

In the early part of the 6th century, about 515, Hygelac, King of the Geats (inhabiting the modern Götaland in southern Sweden), made an incursion upon the Frankish lands along the lower Rhine. The Frankish prince Theudebert met him in desperate battle, and routed him utterly by sea and by land. Hygelac and most of his followers perished, and the booty they were carrying off was retaken. Among the Geats was a young nephew of Hygelac, named Beowulf, a man of extraordinary strength and skill in swimming, who made his escape. The story is well authenticated; it is narrated by Gregory of Tours in his great work, the *Gesta Francorum*. The fame of the battle and of its hero, Beowulf, must have spread not only among the Danes and Swedes but also to England, where it was probably commemorated in popular songs. In the course of time the person of the historic Beowulf became merged in that of the god Beowa, and out of this merging of myth and history, then, has issued our Beowulf poem. The theme was undoubtedly a favorite among the Angles and Saxons. Even after they were converted to Christianity, they preserved the substance of the Beowulf stories intact. But expressions savoring too strongly of heathenism were expunged one by one, and phrases and passages of a distinctively Christian or monkish character were interpolated. It is believed that the Beowulf poem, in very nearly the shape in which we now find it, was committed to writing, probably in Northumbria, about the beginning of the 8th century. The only existing manuscript of it is one of the 10th century, now in the British Museum. It is illegible in several places, having been injured by fire in 1731. The language is West-Saxon.

13. As now printed, the poem contains 3,184 full verses (lines). It reads at first sight like one homogeneous piece; but on closer examination it reveals numerous inconsistencies and interpolations. According to the searching investigations of Professor Müllenhoff, it may be reduced to two primitive and independent stories: first, the fight between Beowulf and Grendel; second, the fight between Beowulf and the fire-dragon. These two stories are of equally ancient origin; but whether composed by one and the same poet, can not be made out with certainty.

The first of the primitive stories is contained in verses

194–836; the second, in verses 2200–3184. All the rest of the poem is, in Müllenhoff's judgment, nothing but secondary matter. Even those sections of the poem which embody the primitive stories themselves are not free from interpolation. Out of a total of 3184 verses, only 930 can rightfully be called 'original,' namely, 490 verses for the first story, 440 for the second.

Thus, the introduction, 1–193, is evidently a late addition, and is a rather clumsy attempt on the part of some secondary verse-maker to set forth the pedigrees, &c., of the chief personages who figure subsequently. The first primitive story begins v. 194. Beowulf, thane of Hygelac, King of the Geats, learns of the troubles of Hrothgar, King of the Danes, and resolves to go to his relief. Hrothgar, namely, having built him a great hall, called Heorot, is grievously molested there by the nightly attacks of a water-monster, Grendel, who kills many of his best knights and carries off others. The description of the voyage of Beowulf and his companions from Geataland to the Danish land, although brief, is spirited. They are graciously received by Hrothgar. When the evening banquet is at an end, Hrothgar and his men retire to the inner rooms, leaving the great hall, which is the scene of Grendel's ravages, in charge of the new-comers. They all fall asleep, except the leader. Grendel sallies forth as usual from his den in the moor, and coming to the hall tears open the door. Light flashes like fire from his eyes. He laughs to himself at the prospect of gratifying his greed of human flesh. But Fate, the 'weird' sister, no longer decrees, literally 'weaves,' that he shall carry off one of human kind after this night. Beowulf, awake, watches him. Quickly the monster falls upon a sleeping Geat and in an instant has torn him to pieces. The next to be attacked is Beowulf. But the hero, bracing himself on his (left) elbow, clutches Grendel with his right hand.

The dragon finds to his dismay that he has never yet en-
countered a man with such a grip. He tries to flee, but
can not; he is held too firmly. Then Beowulf remem-
bers his promise to King Hrothgar. Rising to his full
height, he takes still firmer hold. The dragon's claw is
crushed; again he tries to flee. The hall resounds with
the din, the ale-cups of the Danes clatter to the ground.
It is a wonder that the hall does not shake to pieces;
but it is fastened too strongly within and without with
iron bands wrought with cunning art. Many a bench
is overturned in the desperate fray. The listening
Danes are filled with terror, when they hear the evil one •
utter his cry of defeat; in the naïve wording of the
original, he yells his dreary death-song. Many a fol-
lower of Beowulf hastens to aid with his sword. But
the best of swords would be of no avail against Grendel's enchanted mail. The combatants close in a supreme effort; the dragon's shoulder is wrenched open,
the sinews torn asunder. Victory is with Beowulf.
Grendel, leaving his arm behind, flees mortally wounded
to his den. And Beowulf, in token of victory, hangs
up the dragon's arm and claws under the broad roof.

Here the first story ended, according to Müllenhoff.
It has all the characteristics of an episodic poem; it is
abrupt, concise, straightforward, and intensely vivid.
For power, it is worthy of a place among the treasures
of any people, ancient or modern. It is followed in the
poem by a number of incidents and digressions, the
chief of which are these. The next night there is a
grand banquet, at which costly gifts are bestowed upon
Beowulf by the grateful Hrothgar. The Danes being
left in charge of the hall over night, are attacked by a
second monster, Grendel's mother, who has come to
avenge her son. She carries off Hrothgar's favorite
councillor, Aschere. Once more Hrothgar is disconso-
late. But Beowulf comforts him by promising to attack

the she-monster in her den. He does so, and—after an
even more desperate encounter—kills the mother and
cuts off and brings back the gigantic head of the dead
Grendel himself. Beowulf then returns to his home and
is welcomed by Hygelac.

All this, even including the fight between Beowulf
and Grendel's mother, is pronounced by Müllenhoff to
be mere secondary amplification. But certain discoveries, made since the publication of Müllenhoff's essay,
put the episode with Grendel's mother in a new light.
It has been found that the story of Beowulf's victory
over the two water-demons is contained in Icelandic, in
the *Grettis-saga*, composed not much later than the year
1250. The hero of the *saga*, Grettir Asmundarson, is a
historical personage of the 11th century, an outlaw
noted for his strength and courage. To him has been
transferred, by the imagination of the Icelandic saga-
men, the entire Beowa-myth in the following shape.
Grettir, in requital for hospitality shown him, un-
dertakes to defend a certain house against the night-
attack of 'trolls' by whom it had been disturbed. At
midnight a gigantic woman makes her appearance; the
fight which ensues ends in his cutting off her right arm
with his sword, and the giantess throws herself over a
water-fall near the house and disappears. Some time
afterwards Grettir takes with him the village priest, to
help in exploring this water-fall. The priest fastens a
long rope firmly in the bank, so that the end reaches to
the water at the foot of the fall. Grettir plunges off the
bank into the water, swims up to the fall, and climbing
up some rocks succeeds in making his way into a cavern
behind the sheet of falling water. Here he espies a
huge giant sitting by the fire. A desperate fight ensues,
of course, in which Grettir is again victorious. He kills
the giant, and finds much treasure in the cave, which he

carries off, together with the bones of two men, the giant's victims.

The resemblance between this *saga* and the Old-English poem is too great to be a mere coincidence. We may even say that the story of Grettir explains one or two points in the description of Beowulf's encounter with Grendel's mother, which have been quite obscure until now. And both the Icelandic and the English texts employ one peculiar word which occurs nowhere else in the two languages. Everything indicates that the Icelandic and the English story proceeded from a common original which contained both encounters. All readers of the Beowulf-poem will probably be glad to have the claims of this part to 'originality' successfully vindicated, for it embodies one of the most thrilling episodes —namely, where Beowulf, weary, stumbles and falls. The poet says, simply but powerfully: 'Then sat she upon the hall-guest and drew her short sword, broad, brown-edged; she purposed avenging her bairn, her only offspring. But on his shoulder lay the woven breast-net, protecting the body, refusing an entrance to point and to edge.' Beowulf's armor is woven of links of steel, without any joints or seams through which a sword or a dagger might be thrust.

14. The second primitive story, v. 2200–3184, contained in its original shape about 440 verses, *i.e.*, was about equal in length to the first. It was probably equally vivid. But the interpolations and corruptions of the text are so numerous that it is difficult to give a satisfactory statement of it without going into intricate details. The chief points seem to be these. After the fall of Hygelac and his immediate family in battle, Beowulf becomes king. This total destruction of the direct line of succession is evidently a reminiscence of the overthrow and death of the historic Hygelac.

Beowulf reigns fifty years with great renown. One of his servants, having incurred his anger, flees and hides himself in a cave that he accidentally discovers. The cave proves to be the den of a fire-dragon, who is absent for the moment, and is filled with rare treasures. Hoping to propitiate his master, the servant takes one of them, a costly drinking-cup, and returns home. Beowulf with eleven companions sets out to attack and plunder the cave. But this time he is less successful. On the one hand, the monster is a *fire*-dragon, and therefore more formidable than Grendel; on the other, Beowulf is well on in years and less vigorous. All his followers except one, Wiglaf, desert their master. Wiglaf and Beowulf together succeed at last in killing the dragon, but not until Beowulf has been mortally wounded. Unable to explore the cave himself, he sends Wiglaf in, who comes back loaded with vessels of gold and silver. Making his dying speech, Beowulf nominates Wiglaf his successor. The other knights returning, Wiglaf upbraids them bitterly with cowardice, and bids them prepare for troublous times. Now that their great king is gone, their enemies, the Franks and the Frisians, will not spare them. This passage is doubtless a post-factum prophecy of the breaking-up of the power of the historic Geats. The whole folk is then convened. The corpse of the hero is laid upon a stately pyre, the smoke of which ascends to heaven amid universal weeping and wailing.

Next to the *Nibelungen-lied*, the poem of Beowulf has received the most attention from scholars. Editions of it are numerous; it has been translated into English prose by Kemble, and into modern German alliteration by Grein. Yet despite all such efforts, much of the poem still remains and will probably always remain obscure. Purely descriptive and narrative passages do not offer serious difficulty. But the genealogies, the epic

'asides,' and the passages where an originally heathen
conception or allusion has been effaced to make room
for some monkish moralizing, are enough to puzzle the
wits and weary the patience of the best scholars.

15. Three other heroic poems (or fragments) remain
to be mentioned. The *Fight of Finnsburg* commemorates
an episode which is alluded to in the Beowulf-poem.
Sixty Danes with their leaders, Huaef and Hengest, while
lodged in the castle of Finn, King of the Frisians, are
treacherously attacked by their host. Huaef falls, but
the Danes hold out for five days, when a truce is made.
But it is not kept long. The fighting is renewed and
Hengest and Finn both perish. The beginning of the
piece is very graphic in its abruptness; it describes the
first onslaught. Then exclaimed the king (Hengest),
young in battle : That is not the dawn coming from the
east, neither is it the flight of a dragon, nor the blaze of
the horns of the hall. They are coming to surprise us.
The birds are singing, the cricket chirps, the shields ring,
shield answers to arrow. Now the full moon shineth behind clouds, now start up deeds of woe that the hate of
this folk is minded to do. But arouse you, my warriors,
lift up your hands, be mindful of your might, fight in
the front, be heroes !

The fragment called *Waldere*, in High German ' Wal-
ter,' is connected with the well known continental epic'
of Walther of Aquitaine, preserved in a Latin-hexameter
version of the 10th century. Walther is eloping with
his bride, Hildegund, from the court of Attila, King of
the Huns, when he is intercepted and attacked by Hagen
and Gunther (characters that reappear in another form
in the *Nibelungenlied*). The English *Waldere* proves that
the conquerors of Britain were familiar with the cycle of
Theoderic of Bern (Verona).

The most interesting of these minor pieces is the one
called *Widsith*, or 'Traveler' (literally ' wide-farer ').

In composition it is probably the oldest extant specimen of Anglo-Saxon verse. The chief person, Wídsíth, is a type of the restless, roaming poet-knight of those early days, singing of his wanderings. He tells of Angles and Saxons, Goths, Swabians, Langobards, and Burgundians. What makes the poem peculiarly interesting is that it speaks of many of these peoples, notably the Angles, as still in their early homes before setting out on their migration over the Roman empire.

Of Anglo-Saxon heroic poetry in general it is to be observed that its personages and events all antedate the conquest of Britain. Nowhere do we find an allusion to this great event, or to the exploits by which it must have been attended. In other words, although the poems themselves were put into shape on English soil, the themes must have been brought from the continent. This phenomenon has not yet been sufficiently accounted for. Probably we shall never be able to account for it, unless manuscripts be discovered containing poems now unknown.

CHAPTER V.

CONVERSION TO CHRISTIANITY—BEDE, ALDHELM, BONIFACE.

16. The conversion of the Angles and Saxons to Christianity is the first great event in their history, our knowledge of which rests on a satisfactory basis.

It is the office of the political and ecclesiastical historian to discuss this movement in its details. But the historian of our literature is called upon to show at least how the conversion affected the habits of thought of the people, and gave to it new motives, new hopes and fears, new standards of right and wrong, and new forms of expression.

The Keltic inhabitants of England had accepted Christianity in the times of the Romans. Ireland was converted in the 5th century. The church of Ireland became in the course of the 6th and 7th centuries conspicuous for zeal and learning. Among its leaders may be mentioned Columba, founder of the celebrated monastery of Iona (one of the Hebrides); Gallus, founder of the still more celebrated monastery of St. Gall (Switzerland), and Columbanus, founder of Bobbio (Piedmont). But the Irish church was viewed with some jealousy and mistrust by the general Western church. It was charged with certain quasi heretical tenets, and with want of sufficient deference to the supremacy of the pope. As to the Britains, although they had been converted as early as the 3d century, we know but little of their church, and that little does not inspire respect. It seems to have been a prey to ecclesiastical and political dissensions; the British rulers were given up to intrigues and degrading vices. Yet, feeble as it was, the British church might have developed a healthier life, had it not been hopelessly ruined, together with the British people, by the Anglo-Saxon conquest. At the end of the 6th century a line drawn due south from Abercorn (near Edinburgh) to Weymouth (in Dorsetshire), would have represented not unfairly the two great divisions of the island. All to the east, Germanic and heathen; all to the west, Keltic and Christian, in name at least. The Keltic inhabitants of the greater part of Scotland had been converted in the 6th century by missionaries from Ireland.

The mission of converting the Angles and Saxons was conducted from two sides simultaneously: from the north, by Irish-Scotch missionaries; from the south, by missionaries sent direct from Rome. In the early part of the year 597, Augustine and his companions landed on the shores of Kent. They had been sent by the then pope, Gregory the Great. Ethelberht, ruler of Kent, accepted

the new doctrine. Canterbury became the center of the
Roman Catholic propaganda, and Augustine was consecrated first archbishop. On the north the district of
Northumbria was overrun by missionaries from Iona,
chief among whom was the celebrated Aidan. The
monastery of Lindisfarn (subsequently called Holy Isle),
not far from the mouth of the Tweed, became the centre
of the northern propaganda. The middle portion of the
country, Mercia, under King Penda, held out the longest.
But Penda's defeat by Oswi, King of Northumbria, in
655, sealed the fate of heathenism. Henceforth there
was but one God acknowledged in England, Scotland,
Wales, and Ireland, but one church, and but one faith.
The worship of Thor and of Othin once broken, its fragments were soon swept away, or lingered only as idle,
harmless superstitions among the uneducated lower
classes. The conversion was not only rapid, but thorough; so thorough, indeed, that in little more than a
hundred years, say about the beginning of the 8th century, England became the foremost branch of the church
in western Europe. The prestige and influence of the
Irish church was already on the decline. For this there
were several reasons. The Irish princes were at odds
among themselves, and the island became a prey to Nor-
wegian and Danish pirates.

17. During the 8th and 9th centuries the doctrines of
the Roman Catholic Church became more and more sys-
tematized and its organization perfected. In fact it
ceased to be for the most part a missionary church, and
assumed gradually the character of a highly organized
corporation for the management of public and private
morals, not infrequently also of politics. The aim of the
church, at least in western Europe, was steadily fixed
upon the concentration of its power in the hands of the
pope, and upon the obliteration of everything that sa-

vored of heresy, schism, and national or local dissent.
Italy, Spain, France, Western Germany, and the British
Isles were made distinctively *Roman*-Catholic.
Not even the power of the church could eradicate race-
hatred. In Great Britain, for instance, the Saxon and
the Kelt continued to look upon each other as foes. The
process of conquering and Germanizing the surviving
Britons in western and southwestern England and in
Wales went on for centuries. In the north the Gaels
were crowded farther and farther back into the High-
lands. Yet, as *Christians*, all the races and inhabitants
of the British Isles acknowledged allegiance to Rome
and in so far were on a footing of equality. Moreover,
they were united by at least one bond, viz., the Latin
church-ritual. To us in the 19th century this may not
seem much. But it behooves us to do justice to the past.
Whatever views we may hold of the church of Rome as
it now is, we must not forget that it was the mainstay of
society and of culture from the 3d century to the 13th.
It did what no other power could have done, it taught
the peoples of Europe that they were brothers before
God. Its methods and practices may not seem to us perfectly proper. But it never for an instant lost sight of
its mission, it never forgot that it was the divinely ap-
pointed arbiter between king and king, between nation
and nation. It summoned rulers and subjects before its
tribunal and made them understand that there were such
things as international justice and international sympa-
thies. From the 3d century to the 13th, then, the work
of the church was one of beneficence. But from the
13th century on, we observe symptoms of discontent,
which culminated in the Protestant Reformation of the
16th century.

It does not seem to have cost the Anglo-Saxon people
much of a struggle to give up their heathen gods.
What opposition there was, came chiefly from a few

princes who distrusted the missionaries because they were foreigners. The gods of Germanic mythology were too crude and vague to maintain themselves before the simplicity and unity of the Christian creed. Besides, the old mythology offered no well developed system of ethics. It recognized little virtue beyond brute force and brute valor. It was incapable of suggesting high ideals of daily life. To abjure Othin and worship Christ, then, was a comparatively slight task. The difficulty lay on the other side, in adopting the ritual. The early Britons had accepted Roman priests and a Latin ritual as a matter of course, for Latin was the language of their military rulers. But the Angles and Saxons recognized no such supremacy. Latin was to them a wholly foreign tongue, and—unlike the Britons —they had never had a separate class of priests. They were called upon not only to worship a new God, but to worship him publicly in a language which they could not speak nor even understand, and to consent to the establishment of a close corporation of priests, of whom many, if not most, were at the outset foreigners. Yet hierarchy and ritual were matters in which the church could not afford to make concessions. They were established. Precisely in what way and with what promptness, we are unable to ascertain. All we can say is that through the adoption of Christianity Latin became once more a language of England. It was the sole acknowledged and official language of the church in all matters of doctrine and ritual, and in intercourse between England and the papal see. As the church was in those days the sole depository of learning, Latin became also the vehicle of imparting knowledge. All the teachers were members of the clergy or of religious orders, and all the schools were cathedral or cloister-schools. Text-books were in Latin, and most of the pupils were candidates for the priesthood. Throughout the Middle Ages the church claimed jurisdiction in cases relating to marriage and divorce, parentage, church property, and the validity of oaths. Bishops exercised the functions of judges, and in their courts, officers and counsel were ecclesiastics. Bulls of the pope and decrees of the ecumenical councils, together with the decisions of the pope's court of appeals, supplied the largest share of the ecclesiastical law and rule of procedure. As a matter of course, Latin was the language used in these episcopal courts. What has been said of England will apply with even greater force to the rest of Europe. We can watch this building-up of an elaborate system of church jurisprudence simultaneously all over Europe, until it assumed definite shape in the *Corpus Juris Canonici.* An example being thus set by the church, we need not be surprised to see the political rulers of England enacting and codifying their secular laws—purely Germanic in character—in a Latin form. Deeds for the conveyance and leasing of property, royal edicts, municipal charters, and other private and public documents were drawn up in Latin.

The details of this change may be left to the political historian; its general significance for the history of our literature may be summed up in a few words. Such wholesale use of a foreign idiom drew a sharp dividing line, which had never before existed, between the learned and the unlearned. On the one side there was a small class of secular and clerical dignitaries and officials; on the other, the great mass of peasants and artizans. Both classes spoke, in every-day matters, the vernacular. But the former class had a jargon all to itself, a monkish book-Latin, of which the latter class had no understanding. Thus Latin came to be regarded as more learned, more elegant, more literary. The folk-speech, even at its best, could not claim equality; it was always more or less open to the charge of being vulgar. This state of opinion lasted in England until the Reformation in the 16th century, and even later. Whoever wished to write as a scholar for scholars must perforce write in Latin. English might be good enough for peasants, working-men, soldiers, even for writers of verse and popular tales, but it was not good enough for science. Lord Bacon evidently thought that it was not in the 17th century.

This prevalence of Latin was not an unmixed evil. It established an international language, as the church had established an international code of manners and morals. Men of letters of different countries could converse and correspond with one another. The evil lay chiefly in its retarding the growth of the popular tongue. The church everywhere absorbed the best talents, and the folk-speech was left to be cultivated by men of inferior ability. Herein England will compare most favorably with continental nations, at least in the times anterior to the Norman Conquest. Kings and bishops in England encouraged the translation of useful works from Latin into English, and also the composition of religious pieces in English. The result was that the vernacular literature of England from 750 to 1050 exceeded in volume and importance that of France and that of Germany.

18. It was stated, near the close of § 5, that English thought and speech, even in the earlier heathen period, was marked by a tone of soberness or sadness. This tone was confirmed and deepened by the conversion to Christianity. In becoming Christians, the Angles and Saxons, it is true, did not immediately cease to be pugnacious. There were still feuds enough between neighbor and neighbor, between prince and prince. The so-called Heptarchy might almost be called a period of anarchy. But as time wore on, the supreme power was gradually concentrated in the royal family of Wessex. The habits of the folk became peaceful; so peaceful, in fact, that the land was barely able to defend itself from the Danes. In proportion, then, as the primitive war-like zeal of the folk abated, its tendency to melancholy manifested itself more strongly in its literature. The disposition assumes so many shapes that it is impossible to characterize it in a single word. 'Melancholy' is perhaps too strong. We may call it 'brooding,' or 'yearning,' or 'plaintive.' A musician would probably speak of the religious poetry (about to be mentioned) as composed in the minor key. Not only is its aim didactic—religious poetry can scarcely be otherwise—but it dwells upon the gentle and contemplative moods of the soul, rather than upon the impassioned. Hence it prefers sentiments and reflections to deeds. If we compare, for instance, our early versions of the legends of the saints with the Latin originals from which they were adapted, we shall perceive that the English poet has usually abridged the *action* of the story and sketched to exces-sive length those passages in which the saint gives vent to his feelings. The earliest poems, *e.g.*, the metrical paraphrase of Genesis, § 21, are comparatively free from such diffuseness. But the later we come down, the more of it we shall find. And hand in hand with sentiment-ality of tone goes a fondness for such rhetorical forms as Visions, Dreams, Allegories, and the like. Medieval literature in general exhibits a great variety of visions and allegories, written by ecclesiastics of all nations. But nowhere does this sort of writing appear to have taken such firm hold of the popular imagination as in England. Other European nations, *e.g.*, France and Germany, have produced allegorical and diffusely didactic poets; but England alone pays them peculiar honor. The taste, once acquired, has withstood the Norman Conquest, the Italian Renaissance, and the Protestant

Reformation, and subsists at the present day. We find, in the 14th century, the author of *Piers Plowman* dividing the honors with Chaucer; in the 16th, the *Faery Queen* evershadows every rival; in the 17th, *Pilgrim's Progress* has no rival but *Paradise Lost.* In the 18th century no one poet predominates; and the acknowledged autocrat of letters is Dr. Johnson, not a poet at all but a moral philosopher. In our own time we observe no less a critic than Matthew Arnold asserting that our greatest poet after Shakespeare and Milton is Wordsworth. Many, perhaps most, of us will dissent from this. Yet the mere utterance of the opinion is significant; it reveals the innate bias of the English mind, influencing, some of us would say, *warping* the judgment of our most cultured critic.

Extreme soberness of tone was not the only fault of our pre-Norman literature. It was lacking in color, in grace, in ability to catch the more delicate play of thought and character. And it was also lacking in what is called the ' historic sense.' Having led for centuries a life of comparative isolation, the inhabitants of England were, by the middle of the 11th century, in danger of vegetating in insular exclusiveness. They took no direct active part in the general movement of continental politics. They were absorbed in domestic affairs, and seemed to be disengaging themselves little by little from the great family of nations. In these two respects the changes wrought by the Norman Conquest were not merely salutary but even necessary. For the Normans brought with them from France a fondness for light literature, and also a disposition to enter into foreign politics and to treat the facts and phases of political life in a spirit of philosophic inquiry.

19. The chief seat of the activity of the church in the 8th century was in Northumbria, although the

archbishop of Canterbury was primate of England.
Archbishop Theodore and Abbot Hadrian founded the
celebrated cloister-school of Canterbury near the end of
the 7th century. One of the pupils of the school, Aldhelm, subsequently bishop of Sherborn, directed the
studies in the school of Malmesbury, in Wessex. About
this time Benedict Biscop established the schools of
Wearmouth and Yarrow, in Northumbria, which were
soon to overshadow all the others. Bede, the most illus-
trious name in the annals of the early English church,
was born at Wearmouth in 672, and was educated, partly
there, partly at Yarrow. His whole life was passed in
these two schools, in learning, teaching, and preaching.
He never rose to a higher rank than that of simple
priest. He died, 735, at the age of 62, with the well
earned reputation of being the most learned man of his
times. His life was in the ordinary sense uneventful.
To quote his own words: "I spent my whole life in the
same monastery, and while attentive to the rules of my
order and the service of the church, my constant pleas-
ure lay in teaching, in learning, or in writing." Yet his
fame was European; more than any other one man
probably did he influence the literature of the church.
His scholars numbered upwards of 600, yet he found
time to compose forty-five treatises. The founders
of the monastery having provided a tolerably good library of Latin manuscripts, he had an opportunity of
acquiring a taste for Cicero and Seneca, Ovid and Lucre-
tius. From the followers of Archbishop Theodore of
Canterbury, who was a Greek of Tarsos, he even acquired some knowledge of the Greek language, which
was a very rare accomplishment in those days. The en-
cyclopedic knowledge which he concentrated in himself
and imparted freely to his pupils, or else stored up in
his writings, is justly regarded as the foundation of
scholarship in England.

No less conspicuous than his learning was his personal character. It was so honorable and so attractive that it won for him the designation of "Venerable Bede." There is nothing brighter in the early history of England than the sight of this simple, sweet-tempered priest, filled with love for his fellow-men, gifted with an intelligence far ahead of his times, toiling on patiently and modestly, year after year, in the least obtrusive of vocations.

Bede was fond of his mother-tongue and its verse. Lying on his death-bed he ejaculated, in alliterative lines: Before the inevitable journey no thought can there be more prudent than that man must consider, before his departure, what of good or of evil may be adjudged to his soul after the day of death. Whether the lines were of his own composition or not, is left undecided in the account of his death, written by his friend and disciple, Cuthbert. The same account adds that on the very day of his death he was at work upon a translation of the gospel of John into English, dictating to an amanuensis. Towards evening the young scribe said: "There is yet one more sentence." "Write quickly," replied the dying man. "It is finished now, at last." "You speak truth," said the master, "all is finished." And his spirit passed away, singing the *Gloria in Excelsis.*

None of Bede's writings in the vernacular have been preserved; at least, none in an independent shape, for it is possible that the above-mentioned rendering of the fourth gospel may have been recast subsequently and merged in the general collection of gospel-translations, see § 28. The works of Bede that we possess are in Latin. Those which treat of biblical exegesis and dogmatic theology may be passed over here. But there is one of his works which will interest directly every English-speaking man, viz., his *Historia Ecclesiae Gentis*

Anglorum, a moderate-sized volume narrating the story of the conversion of the Angles and Saxons. Its style is clear, concise, forcible, and remarkably elegant for the 8th century. It is the chief, almost the only, source of our knowledge of the period to which it relates, and it is to this day a very readable book. The simplicity and earnestness of the author are stamped on every page. But not all the parts of the work are of equal value. It is divided into five books. The first twenty-two chapters of Book I give a brief résumé of the history of the island from the invasion by Julius Caesar down to the coming of Augustine in 597. They are a mixture of fact and fable, the latter element predominating. The facts they contain are of no value to us, because our knowledge of them is now derived from independent and better sources. Bede borrowed most of his statements concerning the Romans from Orosius, see § 26. His account of the Britons and the Anglo-Saxon conquest is based upon a Latin treatise, usually called *Gildas*, after its supposed author. This *Gildas* is of such questionable antecedents that we can put no faith in it. Bede's real work begins with the twenty-third chapter. His account of the mission of Augustine and all that follows is undoubtedly authentic. It was based upon documents then existing in England, and upon copies of papal documents, made for him by one of his friends in the archives at Rome. The work ends with a survey of the organization of the English church in the year 731, and a list of the author's writings. A later hand has appended a meagre list of church events, names of bishops, &c., year by year, from 731–766. At the end of one of the manuscripts of the *Historia* are to be found the Northumbrian verses by Caedmon, mentioned § 11, 20. Although Bede's work is in the main genuine history, it is not wholly free from the superstitions in vogue in the Middle Ages. Even Books IV and V, which treat of persons and events contemporary with or just prior to Bede himself, are not wanting in 'visions' and 'wonders.' It is worthy of note that the story of Caedmon, see § 20, is preceded and followed in Book IV by other stories equally marvelous.

One of Bede's contemporaries has been already mentioned, Aldhelm, Bishop of Sherborn and teacher in the school at Malmesbury. Aldhelm lived from about 650 to 709. His reputation for learning was inferior only to that of Bede. Some of his works are in prose, others in verse; they are all of a religious nature except one, a collection of one hundred riddles, imitated from the riddles of Symposius, a late Latin writer of the 4th or 5th century. Although composed chiefly for entertainment, Aldhelm's riddles are rather serious in tone. They are written in various metres, having been designed by their author to serve as illustrations of Latin prosody. For the connection between them and the English riddles of Cynewulf, see § 23.

Aldhelm is said to have been an excellent poet in his mother-tongue, but none of his English pieces have been preserved. By way of compensation we find alliteration in many of his Latin verses. He was also fond of displaying his knowledge of Greek by interlarding his Latin with phrases evidently reproduced from Greek idioms. This trait of pedantry is worth noting; it shows how zealously Greek was studied at that early day in England, and it will moreover prepare us for recognizing the phenomenon that some of the legendary poems of the 8th, 9th, or 10th centuries, in the vernacular of England, see § 25, were based upon primitive Greek versions and not upon secondary Latin ones.

Besides the great schools already mentioned, there was one scarcely less noted, at York. Among the teachers here was Bede's young friend Ecgberht. And in this school was trained the celebrated Alcuin, who afterwards removed to France and became the bosom friend and adviser of Charlemagne, and his assistant in the great plan of reforming education throughout Europe. Another famous Englishman was Winfrid, better known by his Latin name of St. Boniface. After teaching in several schools in his native country, he entered upon his missionary labors in Bavaria, Thuringia, Hesse, Saxony, and Friesland. In 732 he was consecrated archbishop and primate of Germany. He established the bishoprics of Ratisbon, Erfurt, Paderborn, Würzburg, Salzburg, and others, and also the famous abbey of Fulda. It was he who, in 752, at the deposition of Chilperic, the last of the Merowings, consecrated his deposer, Pepin the Short, King of the Franks. The subsequent development of the English church is a matter of general history. Enough has been said in this place to illustrate the promptness and thoroughness of the conversion.

CHAPTER VI.

CHRISTIAN POETRY—CAEDMON—GENESIS, EXODUS, DANIEL.

20. The Christian poetry of early England is scarcely less interesting than the heathen; it is much more abundant, and is easier to interpret. Like the heathen poetry, it is written in alliterative verse. For the survival of heathen notions, see § 6. For the creeping-in of rime, see § 9, § 30. The poets were sometimes monks, sometimes laymen. We have grounds for suspecting that more than one worldly singer, growing weary of wandering and fighting, found refuge and rest within the cloister-walls and sang there of Moses and Abraham as he had formerly sung of Theoderic and Wieland.

First in interest, probably also in time, is the poem

called *Genesis*. It is contained in the Ms. Junian XI., of
the Bodleian library, Oxford, together with three others,
called respectively *Exodus*, *Daniel*, and *Christ and Satan*.
All four poems were formerly ascribed to one author,
namely Caedmon. But at present scholars are agreed
upon the following points. First, that *Christ and Satan*
is much later, both in penmanship and style, than the
other three, and must be assigned to a different era.
Second, that *Genesis*, *Exodus*, and *Daniel*, although written in the manuscript by one and the same scribe, exhibit too much diversity of style and language to be the
work of the same author. The authorship of *Exodus*
and *Daniel* is generally conceded to be unknown. The
only point not yet definitively settled is the authorship
of *Genesis*.

The following story is told by Bede, in his *Historia*,
Bk. IV, ch. 24. In the latter part of the 7th century
(not many years, therefore, before the birth of Bede himself) there lived near the cloister of Streoneshalh (better
known by the subsequent Danish name Whitby) in
Northumbria, a man, well on in years, named Caedmon.
The gift of song had been denied him, so that, when at
table the harp was passed to him in turn, he was wont
to retire in shame. One evening, after being thus dis-
graced, he fell asleep in the stable of which he had
charge. Then appeared to him in his dream a vision,
and a voice called upon him to sing of the beginning of
created things. So he sang in his dream a song in praise
of the Lord, thus: Now shall we laud the author of
heaven, the might of the creator and his counsel, the
deeds of the father of glory, how he, the eternal God,
was the author of all wonders, who first made for the
children of men heaven for a roof, he the holy creator,
and afterwards established the middle region, the earth,
for men, the almighty Lord. Upon awaking, Caedmon
repeated this and added much thereto. The news of the

wonder soon spread to the cloister, where he was called
upon to give specimens of his newly acquired gift. The
abbess Hild received him into the cloister and made her
learned men recite the bible story to him. Whatever
they told him, he elaborated in his mind and turned it
into glorious songs, so that his teachers soon became his
listeners And thus, says Bede, he sang of the creation
of the world and the origin of the human race, and the
whole story of Genesis; of the Exodus of the children
of Israel from Egypt and their entry into the promised
land; of many other sacred stories; of the incarnation
of our Lord, his sufferings, resurrection, and ascension;
of the coming of the Holy Ghost and the preaching of
the apostles; of the terrors of the last judgment and the
pangs of hell and the bliss of heaven. Also many other
songs of God's grace and God's judgments, and in them
all he strove to lead men from sin and incite them to
virtue.

Professor ten Brink, one of the soundest judges of
our early literature, is disposed to concede some basis of
fact to this story, but observes shrewdly that it implies
an extraordinarily wide range of poetic powers and activity. If we take Bede's words literally, this Caedmon
must have been not only an epic but a lyric and a didactic poet of the highest order, and his productions
must have comprised every subject and style of composition in the whole range of our religious poetry. Perhaps we are to regard Bede's Caedmon (like Wídsíth, §
15) as a typical rather than a real character. He seems
to stand for the entire class of humble but zealous con-
verts. Besides, we must remember that the story of
Caedmon is not the only wonder that Bede tells in this
connection, see § 19.

Bede says that he gives only the ' substance ' of Caedmon's dream-song, in Latin prose, beginning thus:
Nunc laudare debemus auctorem regni coelestis, &c. King

Alfred, in his West-Saxon translation of Bede's *Historia*, see § 26, when he comes to this point, uses the following language: Then he (Caedmon) began straightway to sing these words and verses, which he had never heard, the 'order' of which is:

> Nu we sceolon herian   heofonrices weard,
> Metodes mihte   ond his môdgethonc,
>   &c., &c.

In all, nine alliterative full lines, corresponding exactly to Bede's Latin prose.

At the end of one of the Latin MSS. of Bede are found nine lines in the vernacular, beginning thus:

> Nu scylun hergan   hefaenricaes uard,
> Metudaes maecti   end his modgedanc,
>   &c., &c.

The difference between the two sets of verse is merely one of dialect. King Alfred's passage is in Wessex, the other in Northumbrian, but otherwise the two passages agree absolutely.

But the beginning of the Junian *Genesis* (which is also in Wessex dialect) is different, and is worded thus:

> Us is riht micel   thaet we rodera weard,
> Wereda wuldorcining   wordum herigen
> Môdum lufien: he is maegna spêd,
>   &c., &c.

Which may be rendered: It is our bounden duty that we the lord of glory, the wonder-king of peoples, with our words should praise, with our hearts should love; he is the promoter of strength, &c.

The question naturally suggests itself: In what relation do the Latin prose lines in the text of Bede, the Northumbrian verses appended to Bede, and King Alfred's verses stand to one another, and how are they all three related to the poem of *Genesis?*

The problem is complicated, and some of the points

are still in dispute. But opinion seems to be gradually
settling down to these conclusions: 1. That the Latin
MS. of Bede is of the early part of the 8th century, say
737. Consequently it was penned almost immediately
after Bede's death. 2. That the metrical fragment in
Northumbrian appended to this MS. is of the same date
as the body of the MS. 3. That Bede's Latin 'nunc
laudare debemus,' &c., is translated from the Northumbrian. 4. That King Alfred's verses are merely a later
Wessex form of the same Northumbrian. We have in
this Northumbrian fragment, then, the remains of a very
old poem of the 7th century, which nothing prevents us
from ascribing to the Caedmon of whom Bede writes.
The further point, viz., the relation between the Northumbrian fragment and the Junian *Genesis* is not yet
fully cleared up. Probably we shall be safe in taking a
middle position. We may assert, on the one hand, that
the Junian *Genesis* is not a direct Wessex version of the
Northumbriam poem of which the Bede MS. has preserved a fragment. On the other hand, we may admit
that the substance of the early Northumbrian poem has
been embodied in the Junian *Genesis*. According to
Professor ten Brink, the style of *Genesis* gives unmistakable evidence of high antiquity. It suggests an art
of versification in its infancy, not on the decline.

21, *Genesis*, as we have it in the Junian MS., is a
poem of 2935 full verses. Originally it must have been
much longer, for there are six large gaps in the MS., and
the narrative ends abruptly at the sacrifice of Isaac.
The MS. is of the 10th century, but the language is that
of the 9th, if not earlier.

We have to distinguish in the poem two portions of
unequal length and dissimilar character. Namely,
verses 245 to 851 are an interpolation. See § 5. Professor Sievers, who established this fact in the year 1875,

regards the interpolated passage as an English translation from an Old-Saxon poem on the same subject, now
lost, and composed in the latter half of the 9th century,
probably by the author of the famous Old-Saxon *Heliand*. Professor ten Brink has given to the interpolated
passage the title of *Younger Genesis*, and to the older
and main portion the title of *Elder Genesis*.

The poem opens with an invocation to God, and proceeds to sing of the bliss of the angels in heaven and the
rebellion and fall of the angels. These notions concerning the ten orders of angels and the rebellion of Lucifer
are wholly foreign to the bible-text, and are derived from
the writings of Gregory the Great and the compendium
made by Isidor from the writings of Gregory and St.
Augustine. They recur with endless variation all
through medieval literature, see § 24. The poem goes
on to state that after the bad angels have been thrust
out of heaven and peace restored, the Lord is moved
with sorrow at the sight of so many vacant seats. By
way of compensation he proceeds to create earth and
man. The description of the creation conforms strictly
to the bible, except that the two accounts of man's creation (Gen. i. 26; ii. 7) are thrown into one. Some of
the passages are extremely forcible. In describing the
creation of light, the poet bursts forth:

> The earth was yet,
> The grass all ungreen; the sea covered
> By swarthy night far and wide,
> The wan waves. Then came beaming in glory
> The spirit of heaven's warder borne o'er the waves
> With mighty blessing. The lord of the angels,
> The giver of life, bade the light come forth
> Over the wide ground; quickly was obeyed
> The high king's behest. Holy light
> Was over the wastes, as the worker commanded.

The first part of the *Elder Genesis* stops at v. 245, with
the naming of the four rivers of Paradise, Gen. ii. 14.

Passing over the *Younger-Genesis* interpolation for the present, we find the elder poem resuming the story at the point where the Lord calls to Adam in Paradise just after Adam and Eve have eaten the forbidden fruit, Gen. iii. 9. The poet adheres closely to the text. Occasionally he abridges a pedigree; occasionally, on the other hand, he amplifies a passage in accordance with Old-German notions. Thus his description of the flood, although not much longer than that in the original, creates the impression that it must have been adapted to the experience of a sea-faring people. The flood becomes more of a tempest.

The *Younger-Genesis* interpolation is interesting in more than one respect. It repeats, but in a much fuller form, the fall of the angels, and introduces the temptation and fall of man. It describes the fallen angels as they lie bound in the fire of the bottomless pit. Their leader, Satan, delivers a speech in which he declares his unconquered hate and announces his intention to ruin the newly created race of man. The resemblance between this Old-English Satan and Milton's archfiend is striking. But the most significant trait in the interpolated passage is the peculiar character it gives to the temptation. In the bible and in all the ecclesiastical literature of the middle ages Adam and Eve are represented as overcome by the evil spirit's appeal to their idle curiosity or some such improper feeling.

Here, the tempter is a veritable father of lies. He announces himself as a messenger sent from God to *command* them to eat of the tree of knowledge, and threatens them with divine wrath if they refuse. This course places the conduct of our first parents in a better light; it diminishes their guilt, if it does not remove it altogether. It is contrary to the rigorous doctrine of the medevial church, which sought to enhance its own efficacy by deepening man's sinfulness. The only work in which we find a like disposition to touch lightly upon sin and the fall is in the Old-Saxon poem of the *Heliand*, above mentioned. We may account for such a disposition by assuming that the Old-Saxons, who had just been forcibly converted to Christianity by Charlemagne, were unwilling to accept the doctrine of total depravity because it seemed to them an unmanly belief.

22. The next poem in the Junian Ms. is called *Exodus.* This title is too extensive for the matter, which does not include all the events in the biblical Exodus, but merely the march of the children of Israel through the Red Sea and the destruction of the Egyptian army. It is only 589 verses long; at verse 445 there is a gap of two pages in the ms. According to Professor ten Brink, the author must have been an epic singer turned bible-poet and retaining his old love for heroes and weapons. Nowhere in the Christian poetry is the love of fighting so marked. This is all the more striking as the narrative does not have any battle to describe, but can merely tell of preparations for battle and the great danger threatening the Hebrews. The descriptions are more detailed than in Genesis, more imaginative, and more poetical.

The third poem, *Daniel*, contains 765 verses; there is one considerable gap in the ms. Like *Exodus*, it does not give all the contents of the biblical book; it ends abruptly at Dan v. 22, in the midst of the prophet's interpretation of Belshazzar's dream. It selects only important incidents, especially such as inculcate submission to God and trust in him, and distrust of one's own powers. The style is simpler and less graphic than that of *Exodus.*

The last poem of this ms., usually called *Christ and Satan*, is not one homogeneous piece, but is a mere collection, carelessly put together, of fragments of three

separate poems, treating respectively of the pangs of the
Fallen Angels, Christ's Descent into Hell and Ascension,
and Christ's Temptation. All three fragments are evidently much later in date than *Genesis*, *Exodus*, and
Daniel, and also much inferior.

Not much if any later than *Exodus* and *Daniel* are
various short pieces, e.g. a metrical paraphrase of the
50th psalm (in the Kentish dialect), a poem on the Day
of Judgment, descriptions of Hell and Heaven, and the
speeches of the Soul to the Body after Death.

These last mentioned pieces, one for the condemned
soul, one for the blessed soul, exemplify the curious
medieval belief that the soul after death, see § 26, visits
the body every week, until the two shall be reunited at
the judgment-day and consigned together to final bliss
or final woe. There is no lack of similar pieces, prose
and verse, in the medieval literature of every European
nation.

Equally curious are the traces of so-called 'animal
symbolism.' In the earlier centuries of the Christian
era it became a custom among Christians to regard certain animals as symbolizing certain mysteries of the faith.
Compendiums were made for ready reference; such a
compendium was called a *physiologus*. We possess remains of an Anglo-Saxon *physiologus* in the short poems
which treat of the panther and the whale, and in the
fragment of a poem on a curious bird entitled by Grein
'The Partridge.' The Panther, who retires to a se-
cluded spot in the mountain-valley, sleeps three days, and
on awaking utters sweet cries and exhales a delicious
odor, symbolizes Christ, the risen Lord. The Whale,
who beguiles unwary mariners into mistaking him for
an island and climbing on his back, only to open his
jaws and devour them, symbolizes Hell. We find rem-
iniscences of superstitious belief in such treacherous
floating islands even in modern literature.

CHAPTER VII.

CYNEWULF—RIDDLES, CHRIST, ELENE, &C.

23. The person and writings of Caedmon, see § 20, are involved in uncertainty. But our knowledge of another of the great poets of early England is somewhat more definite. Cynewulf was born about the middle of the 8th century. He is usually held to be a native of Northumbria. He belonged in early life to the class of singers who wandered from court to court. His education had been got at a convent-school; at all events he had some knowledge of Latin.

Only one of his secular works has been preserved, viz., a collection of riddles in alliterate verse. The suggestions for these riddles he borrowed partly from Aldhelm, see § 19, partly from oral traditions of the folk. The Angles and Saxons, like the other Germans, had an inborn liking for oracular utterances and plays on words. One of the most celebrated encounters of wit is that narrated in the Vafthrudnismal of the elder Edda. Here the god Othin, assuming the form of a man and the name Gangradr, visits the giant Vafthrudnir in his hall. The two propound to each other the most difficult riddles, until at last Gangradr asks the giant what Othin had whispered in the ear of Balder when the latter was ascending the funeral pile. At this the giant perceives that his antagonist is none other than the father of the gods and acknowledges himself overcome. His head is the forfeit. In this respect the Eddaic story resembles the Greek myth of Oedipus and the Sphinx.

Cynewulf's riddles are marked by imagination, a close observation of nature and the realities of life, and also a relish for social enjoyment. The following may serve as a specimen :

> Me a while ago for dead gave up
> My father and mother; I had no body as yet,
> Nor life within. Then a woman began,
> Well disposed, to cover me with garments,
> Kept and cherished me, enfolded me
> As faithfully as she did her own bairns,
> Until, under her lap, as my nature was,
> Under her foster lap I waxed in spirit.
> Me the protectress fed then
> Until I grew and was able
> To fly afar. She had the less
> Of sons and daughters of her own for thus doing.
>
> [Answer: A Cuckoo.

Cynewulf, it is believed, passed the latter part of his life in a convent. His subsequent writings are all of a religious character. The poem called *Christ*, containing 1690 verses, is composed in three parts: first, the Birth of Christ; second, the Ascension; third, the Coming at the Last Day. (Of part first the beginning is lost.) According to Professor ten Brink the substance of the poem is taken from Latin homilies, especially from those of Gregory the Great. The effect of the whole is that of a cycle of hymns, but liberally intermixed with epic and dramatic elements. In form it passes back and forth from narration to dialogue, from dialogue to ejaculations of praise. To quote Professor ten Brink's words, it is a majestic monument of deep religious feeling and keen, lofty intellect. The feeling of love and adoration for Christ and the Virgin reaches the highest pitch of expression, but without breaking into that sentimental strain which the later Christian poets of the 12th and 13th centuries caught from the *Minnesinger*. Nowhere is the love of Christ described more earnestly, more touchingly, nowhere are the terrors of the last judgment depicted more forcibly. Among all our early

English poems of religion, Cynewulf's *Christ* is the one in which the spirit of the Latin church is exhibited at its best. On the other hand the Old-German conception of the *comitatus*, retinueship, or vassalage, is conspicuous, and we even seem to detect here and there a faint echo of those old pagan hymns that once must have celebrated the glories of Othin's Walhalla.

24. The best known and most popular of Cynewulf's works is the *Elene*, a legendary story of the expedition sent by the emperor Constantine to recover from the Holy Land the cross upon which Christ was put to death. The poem contains 1321 verses; the last 85 are personal. In them the poet speaks of himself as having been troubled in spirit at the recollection of a misspent life, until he is comforted by the contemplation of the Cross and its glory. He then introduces a passage in which, line by line, the runic names of the single letters composing his name are made to bear the alliteration and thus reveal the author. The passage has the effect of an acrostich.

The story of the Finding of the Cross is one of the most interesting and characteristic legends of the early church, and has been preserved in a great variety of versions in many languages. In Cynewulf's version the main points are these. In the year 233 Constantine, still a heathen, is attacked by his enemies, chiefly the Huns. (The date 233 is, of course, impossible. By slightly changing the order of words in Anglo-Saxon, we can get 332, which would come much nearer to the probable date of the emperor's conversion. But the Latin original followed by Cynewulf has the same figures, 233.) In his sleep, on the eve of the battle which is to decide the fate of his empire, an angel of the Lord appears and bids him shake off fear and look aloft for a sign of victory. He looks and beholds in the sky a glit-

tering cross bearing the inscription: With this sign
shalt thou conquer thy enemies. (A translation of the
familiar *in hoc signo vinces*.) Awaking, the emperor orders a cross to be made immediately and carried before
him. Wherever this cross is borne in the fight, the
enemy is dismayed and routed. Having gained a complete victory, Constantine summons his wise men and
bids them interpret this unknown symbol. They are at
a loss for an answer. But at last some Christain soldiers
venture to tell the story of Christ's life and death. The
emperor accepts joyfully the new doctrine and is baptized. Being further instructed in bible-history, he
learns that Christ was put to death in Judea. There-
upon he fits out an expedition, at the head of which he
puts his mother Helena, to find if possible where the
Cross had been hid. As soon as the empress reaches
Jerusalem, she convenes the wise men learned in the
law of Moses. They evade in various ways her persist-
ent questionings. After meeting them thus four times
without success, she throws one of their number, Judas,
into prison and keeps him there six days without food.
On the seventh day his resolution gives way and he
promises to aid in the search.

He guides the Christians to Calvary, but is unable to
find the spot where the Cross has been hid. In his
emergency he prays to God. This prayer, says Professor ten Brink, is a curious blending of Old-Hebrew
fervor and Old-German pathos, tinged with Talmudic
ideas of a hierarchy of angels surrounding the glory of
the Father, § 21. He begs that the spot may be indi-
cated by a cloud of smoke. His prayer is granted. He
returns thanks, and they dig down twenty feet, when
they discover *three* crosses. That is, they have found
also the two on which the thieves were put to death.
Returning to the city, they lay the three before the empress, who rejoices with them but wishes to know which

is the Savior's. Judas is completely at fault. They sing hymns to God until the ninth hour, when a company of mourners pass by, carrying to the grave the body of a young man. Judas orders them to stop and set the bier down. He holds, one after the other, two of the crosses over the corpse; but it remains motionless as before. He then holds the third cross; instantly the dead man arises, body and soul re-united.

Messengers are sent to Constantine to inform him of the discovery. He returns word to erect a church on the spot where the cross was found. The cross is set in gold and precious stones and deposited in the church, in a silver casket. Judas is baptized. By order of the empress, Bishop (Pope) Eusebius of Rome visits Jerusalem and consecrates Judas bishop of the new diocese. Henceforth Judas is known as Cyriacus.

But Helena is not yet satisfied. She wishes to have the nails with which the feet and hands of the Savior were pierced. Once more Cyriacus proceeds to Calvary and prays. A bright flame shoots out of the ground. The nails are dug up and brought to the empress. Cyriacus advises her to have them made into a bit for the emperor's bridle; so long as the emperor shall guide his horse with this bit, so long shall he be victorious. The empress remains a while longer in Jerusalem, helping to build up the new Christian community. Cyriacus performs many miracles of healing. At her departure the empress bestows rich gifts on him and enjoins the church to celebrate the anniversary of the day on which the cross was found. It was the last day but six of spring. As summer began on the 9th of May, according to the Anglo-Saxon calendar, this day would be the 3d of May.

25. Another of Cynewulf's poems, *Juliana,* narrates the martyrdom of a noble Christian woman of that name, supposed to have lived in the reign of the Roman emperor Maximinian. Juliana refuses to wed a heathen husband, and for her steadfast resistance is frightfully tortured and put to death. Cynewulf's version is adapted from the Latin.

The metrical *Life of St. Guthlac* is only in part the work of Cynewulf. It tells of the trials and temptations of Guthlac, a hermit of England, who died 714. Cynewulf's share, the latter part, follows closely a Latin life of the saint by the monk Felix of Croyland.

These four works, viz., the *Riddles*, *Christ*, *Elene*, and *Juliana*, with the portion of *Guthlac*, are all that can be safely claimed for Cynewulf. Several other works were formerly ascribed to him, which are now disputed, viz: *Andreas*, *The Phoenix*, *The Vision of the Rood*, and various shorter pieces. *The Vision of the Rood* is rather a feeble copy of the conclusion of Cynewulf's *Christ* (see beginning of § 24) than a work by the same author. It is monotonous and verbose. *Andreas* is the legendary (and extremely fabulous) story of the adventures and suffering of St. Andrew, who is sent by God to rescue St. Matthew from captivity in the land of the Mermedons. The poet, whoever he may have been, followed a Greek, not a Latin, version, as is shown by certain peculiar locutions. *The Phoenix*, a poem of 677 verses, is a metrical rendering of a Latin poem ascribed to Lactantius, a church-father of the 4th century. Herodotus, who got the fable from the Egyptians, was the first to tell of this wonderful bird. The next writer of importance was Ovid. During the first century of the Christian era two slightly different versions sprang up. According to one, when the phoenix dies, a new bird arises from the dead body and buries it. According to the other, the phoenix burns himself, and a new bird arises from the ashes. The latter version is more usual, and is the one followed by Lactantius in his *De Phoenice* and by our early English poet. But the English poem, from v. 380 on, develops an idea which is not in the Latin original at all, *i.e.*, it applies the phoenix-myth to the Christian doctrine of the resurrection. The new-born phoenix is made to symbolize the risen Lord and the elect. This added part is of course the most interesting.

Among the minor poems of this period, although not to be connected with Cynewulf, are *The Lament of Deor*, remarkable for its being the only poem composed in strophes (or stanzas), *The Wanderer*, *The Seafarer*, *The Ruin*, *The Message of the Husband to his Wife*, and a collection of pithy sayings, usually called 'gnomic' verses. All except the gnomic verses are marked by a strong undercurrent of sadness. It is impossible to discover their authors, or even to determine accurately the times when they were composed. But in all probability they are anterior to the reign of King Alfred.

CHAPTER VIII.

KING ALFRED—OROSIUS, BOETHIUS, PASTORAL CARE— CHRONICLE.

26. Mention has been made in § 11 of the troubles caused in the early part of Alfred's reign by the Danish invasions. In 878 a treaty was concluded at Wedmore, which practically divided England into a northeastern portion under Danish overrule, and a southwestern, Wessex, under Alfred.

Having conquered peace, Alfred bent his energies to the task of repairing the terrible damages that had been wrought. He paid as much attention to restoring p ety and learning as to political and military reform. Not content with rebuilding and endowing schools and churches, he set in his own person an extraordinary example of unceasing literary activity. Late in life he began the study of Latin and translated numerous works into the vernacular. Nearly all his writings have been preserved. They fully establish his claim to be regarded as the father of our English prose.

The first work that he translated was a Latin history of the world, composed about 418 by a Spanish monk named Orosius. The Latin original is a mere compilation, immethodical and uncritical. But it has one merit; it is the first attempt to write history from an international point of view. Its spirit is orthodox-christian, but its tone, we might say, is cosmopolitan. It is certainly not exclusively Greek or exclusively Latin. The seven books of Orosius were a favorite work throughout the early middle ages. We have seen, § 19, that Bede consulted them. In translating the first chapter of the first book, Alfred inserted some materials of his own, viz., a description prepared by himself of all the countries that were then occupied by German-speaking tribes, and two reports of exploring voyages, written down by him from the dictation of the men who had made the voyages. Ohthere, starting from his home on the western coast of Norway, had doubled the North Cape and explored the White Sea as far as the mouth of the river Dwina. He was undoubtedly the first man of Germanic descent to discover those regions. The other traveler, Wulfstan, starting from what is now the town of Sleswig, explored the coast of the Baltic as far as Danzig and Königsberg. These two reports and Alfred's description are the most interesting and valuable contributions that we possess to the ethnography of the times.

Alfred's next translation was from Bede's *Historia*, see § 19. This was followed by a free rendering of the celebrated work by Boethius, *De Consolatione Philosophiae*. Boethius, often called the 'Last of the Romans,' was a prominent statesman and philosopher of the 6th

century.   Being charged, unjustly it is now believed,
with complicity in a conspiracy against the Gothic king,
Theoderic, he was thrown into prison and finally executed,
525.   It was during his imprisonment that he composed
his *Consolatio*.   The work is in the main an embodiment
of Neo-Platonic doctrines, but with a considerable ad-
mixture of Stoicism.   Its Christianity is rather superfi-
cial, for Boethius was only a Christian in name.   But by
reason of its clear and elegant style and the good sense
of its teachings, it became almost immediately a popular
work among churchmen and exerted a wonderful influence upon all medieval writers, lay no less than clerical.
Chaucer, for instance, never wearies of citing Boethius,
and for several centuries after Chaucer we may observe
the *Consolatio* still maintaining its hold upon men of
learning.   Alfred's translation, or rather paraphrase, can
make no pretense to the elegance of the original.

The work upon which Alfred bestowed most pains is
the translation of Pope Gregory's *Pastoral Care*, a
treatise by the great pope upon the true nature of the
priestly vocation and the proper way of fulfilling its
duties.   Gregory's teachings were peculiarly applicable
to the English clergy in Alfred's reign, who were very
imperfectly trained.   Hence the King ordered a copy of
his translation to be kept in every cathedral church of
his realm.   Two of these very manuscripts still remain ;
one is much injured, the other is entire except a single
leaf at the end.   They exhibit the actual language of the
south of England in the 9th century, as it was written
down under the eyes of the King, and are consequently
of the highest philological value.   Alfred's Preface, in
the form of a letter to Bishop Werferth, gives a forcible
account of the disorganization and ignorance of the
country during the early part of his reign, and the energetic measures he employed to disseminate knowledge.

Another work of Gregory's, the so-called *Dialogues*,

was not translated by Alfred himself, but by his friend Werferth, bishop of Worcester. These *Dialogues* embody the views of the pope upon the lives and miracles of the early Italian saints. They owe their title to the circumstance that they are put into the shape of a series of imaginary conversations between Gregory and his archdeacon Peter. The fourth (last) book exerted a remarkable influence upon medieval literature. It treats of the life of the soul after death, see § 22, and recounts many of the 'visions' of spiritual and supernatural things vouchsafed to holy men in the early church. Closely connected with the visions was the doctrine of 'purgatory,' which was in process of establishment in Gregory's day. From Gregory's Latin *Dialogues* these visions and purgatorial wonders passed into early Irish literature, where they were developed freely and transfused with Keltic superstition, f rming a department by themselves. The doctrine of purgatory became permanently associated with the name of Patrick, the patron saint of Ireland. As retold and modified by Irish monks, the literature of visions spread over all Europe, assuming a more popular shape in the Arthurian romances.

27. For a statement of the general relations between Wessex and Northumbria, in the matter of prose and poetry, see § 11.

Wessex is entitled to the additional credit of having originated the beginnings of national historiography in the vernacular. It had long been a custom among monks throughout Europe to jot down, in Latin, year by year, brief notices of important events, such as royal births, deaths, marriages, great battles, and other changes, especially in the monastic order itself and in the church. These notices are usually as meagre and matter-of-fact as memoranda entered in a private diary. But it seems that the monks of Canterbury and Winchester must have begun at an early date to write their notices, not in Latin but in the vernacular. During the reign of Ethelwulf, Alfred's father, the first attempt was made to work up these scattered items into something like a continuous narrative. The history of the Angles and Saxons was carried back to the days of Hengist and Horsa, and King Ethelwulf's pedigree traced through Othin to Noah and Adam. All that part of this first Winchester *redaction* which deals with persons and events anterior to the 7th century is of questionable value, and is probably, to a large extent, mere popular tradition. Passages here and there read like scraps of ancient poetry turned into prose. But the part dealing with the 7th century and 8th century is authentic, being probably taken in substance from early monkish records.

Towards the end of Alfred's reign the annals underwent a second redaction, which continued the thread of narrative down to 891. The new matter consists chiefly of the events of Alfred's wars with the Danes, and has therefore all the value of a contemporary record. But those who had the second redaction in charge interpolated a good many passages in the preceding part, *i.e.*, in the fabulous history of early Britain. They carried the narrative back as far as 60 B. C. These interpolations are not taken from popular tradition but from Bede's *Historia*. Probably the respect thus shown to Bede was due to King Alfred's wishes.

After Alfred's death the record was resumed—we can not say where or by whom—and continued to 924, the year in which Alfred's son, Edward, was at the height of his power and ruler over nearly all England. Professor ten Brink ascribes this entire section of thirty years, 891–924, to the pen of a single writer, who must have been a man of great ability and the best prosaist of Old-England. His style is unusually clear and vigorous.

The annals for the next half century, 924–975, are

meagre and dry. They are enlivened only by the insertion of four episodes, narrated in alliterative verse. First, the victory of Athelstan over the Scotch and Northmen, at Brunanburh; second, the annexation of the five Danish 'boroughs' of Leicester, Lincoln, Nottingham, Stamford, Derby, 924; third, Edgar's coronation at Bath, 973; fourth, Edgar's death, 975.

About 1000 the annals seem to have been transferred from Winchester to Canterbury, Worcester, and Abingdon. In Worcester, about 1016, a further redaction was made, by interpolating many facts and dates relating to Northumbria and Mercia, which had been collected in the course of the 9th and 10th centuries. Another redaction was made in Abingdon, about 1046. The two versions, the Worcester and the Abingdon, then continue, between them, the story of England under the Danish king Knut, under Edward the Confessor, Goodwin, and Harold, down to the battle of Hastings.

After the Norman Conquest, composition of every sort in the language of the conquered was neglected. The annals merely shared in the general decay, until at last they died a natural death, 1154, when Henry II. ascended the throne. The additions made from 1066–1154 are meagre enough. Some were made at Canterbury; a few more at Worcester. The principal redaction of this period was made at Peterborough. In 1116 the cathedral and nearly all the adjacent buildings, with their books and other documents, were destroyed by fire. This furnished the occasion for rewriting the entire record. The writers consulted the earlier records of Winchester, Worcester, Canterbury, and Abingdon; also the local records of Peterborough. They interpolated some forged charters purporting to convey gifts to the abbey, and brought the story down to 1121. From 1121–1131 this Peterborough record was kept up year by year.

The section from 1132–1154, as it now stands, was probably added by a single scribe, in 1154.

The entire record, whether early or late, whether prepared at Winchester, Canterbury, Worcester, Abingdon,
or Peterborough, is usually entitled the *Anglo-Saxon
Chronicle.* It is in the main dry and tedious reading,
imperfect, abrupt, not always intelligible or accurate.
Yet it is a most valuable document to the historian and
to the grammarian; it is moreover worthy of honor for
being the first great and sustained effort on the part
of a modern folk to tell its own history in its own speech.

CHAPTER IX.

ALFRIC—SOLOMON & SATURN, &C.—DECLINE OF POETRY.

28. For the sake of unity, all the parts of the Anglo-
Saxon Chronicle have been mentioned in § 27, although
many of them belong in point of time to the present
chapter.

The literature of England from the death of Alfred
to the Norman Conquest is more abundant than the
earlier literature, but is in general much less interesting.
It is almost altogether a prose literature, and is dry and
didatic in style. It bears witness to the dying out of the
great creative impulse in poetry.

Among the more curious productions of the period is
the *Laece Boc* (Leech Book), a compilation of rules and
prescriptions for the treatment of various diseases. As
might be expected from the low state of medical study in
the middle ages, the compilation swarms with fantastic
notions. Many forms of disease are attributed to evil
spirits, for which the cure consists in incantations and ex-
orcisms. Some of the formulas are in verse, and date

perhaps from heathen times. Not a few of the superstitions still survive among English rustics. The *Laece
Boc* is based upon a Latin compilation, supposed to be
the work of one Apulejus, a Roman physician of the last
days of the Empire.

The chief prose writings are of a religious character,
and may be regarded as a continuation of the work of
instruction begun by Alfred. The great reformer of the
10th century was St. Dunstan, Archbishop of Canterbury, whose efforts were directed to winning back the
priests from worldly amusements, to enforcing celibacy
among them, and to establishing the strict rule of St.
Benedict in the monasteries. But St. Dunstan has left no
writings in English. What he neglected to do, was more
than made good by Alfric, Abbot of Ensham. Alfric,
who died about 1020, was a pupil of the celebrated
school at Winchester and the most indefatigable writer
of his times. The more important of his works are:
1. A collection of 80 and more homilies, entitled *Catholi-
cae.* • 2. An interlinear version of selections from Pris-
cian's Latin grammar, and an interlinear *Colloquium*, or
dialogue between teacher and pupil, so planned as to
facilitate the learning of Latin words and phrases. 3. A
collection of homilies on the lives of the saints, entitled
Passiones Sanctorum. 4. A translation of the Pentateuch
(omitting passages here and there), of Joshua, Judges,
and Job. 5. An Introduction to the Study of the Old
and New Testament. Several of these writings are in
alliteration, *e.g.*, the greater part of the *Passiones*, and
the books of Numbers, Joshua, and Judges. The alliteration is, to say the least, a mistake on the author's
part. It has not the power of the old heathen poetry
nor the grace of Cynewulf's poetry. It does not con-
form to the rules of alliterative verse; in fact it is little
more than slightly versified prose, and is much inferior
to his regular prose. But, notwithstanding this weak-

ness, Alfric was the model of an industrious scholar, and indisputably the most influential writer of English after King Alfred. The above list gives but a fraction of his numerous writings.

Somewhat earlier in time than Alfric is the Northumbrian interlinear version of the gospels, made in Lindisfarn and transferred to Durham when that city became the seat of the bishopric. Also earlier than Alfric by a few years is a collection of homilies preserved in the Blickling MS. Later probably than Alfric, certainly not by him, is the Wessex translation of the gospels.

29. An interesting poem of this period is one entitled *Solomon and Saturn.* Solomon symbolizes Christian, Saturn heathen wisdom; the poem is in the form of a dialogue or encounter of wits, in which—as might be expected—Solomon comes off victorious. The theme was a favorite one in the middle ages; but, although it must have originated in the east, we have no version, Latin, Greek, or otherwise, earlier than the Anglo-Saxon. Solomon as representative of christian doctrine calls for no explanation. But it is not so easy to account for the introduction of Saturn. It is believed that there was a Jewish tradition according to which Solomon figured as the champion of Jewish wisdom against Marcolis, an oriental divinity corresponding to the classic god Mercury. Among German-speaking nations the oriental name Marcolis was converted into Marculf; and this form is still retained in the continental-German versions of the story. But in England the name Marcolis seems to have been confounded with Malcol (Milcol), *i.e.*, Moloch, the name of another oriental divinity corresponding to Saturn. Thus the word Saturn came to be substituted in England for Marculf. The old English version is quite fragmentary, and—like all mystical writings—is obscure. A large part of it consists in Solo-

mon's going through the *Pater Noster* for Saturn's edifi-
cation, interpreting each letter as if it were a rune. The
continental versions, notably the French, differ from the
English in giving to the dialogue a burlesque tone, and
the wit not infrequently becomes profane and scurrilous.

Another and more important production is the metrical paraphrase of the book of Psalms, made not later
than the middle of the 10th century. (An earlier version of the 50th Psalm has been mentioned, § 22). For
the songs inserted in the Chronicle, see § 27. Superior
in every way to these chronicle-songs is one composed
near the end of the 10th century. It is a poem of 325
verses, (both introduction and conclusion are wanting),
in commemoration of Byrhtnoth, and is called either
Byrhtnoth's Death or *The Battle of Maldon*. In the year
991 a band of Northmen landed on the eastern coast of
England. They were attacked near Maldon by Byrhtnoth at the head of a few hastily gathered troops. The
contest was long and desperate. Byrhtnoth fell, but the
invaders were checked. The poem is one of the most
spirited in the language and fully worthy of a place beside
Beowulf and the *Battle of Finnsburh*. It must have been
composed immediately after the battle, for the author
appears not to have known the name of the Danish
leader, which is given as Anlaf in the *Chronicle*.

30. The poetry of the 11th century exhibits unmistakable signs of a transition period. It is the business
of the grammarian to examine these changes in detail.
All that can be attempted in this place is to mention
some of the most marked. 1. The alliteration becomes
more and more careless; almost any similarity of sound
is regarded as sufficient. 2. Less care is taken to let the
alliteration rest on the emphatic words in the line. 3.
There is a tendency to make the transitions of meaning
coincide with the end of the full line. This is in direct

opposition to the style of the earlier poetry, which
usually carries the syntactic meaning over from one line
to the next. Inasmuch as the caesura, or half-way
pause, is still kept up, the full line is thus divided mo-
notonously into two halves. 4. These halves are frequently made to rime. This is a decisive step towards
the riming eight-syllable or ten-syllable ' couplets ' which
were the predominant metre of France and Germany
from the 10th to the 14th century. The following passage, taken from the *Chronicle,* sub anno 1036, will make
all these points clear. It describes the fate of Alfred,
son of Ethelred.

Sôna swâ he lende,   on scype mon hine blende
And hine swâ blindne   brohte to tham munecon,
And he thaer wunode   thâ hwile the he leofode.
Syththan hine man byrigde,   swa him wel gebyrde,
Aet tham westende   tham stypele ful-gehende
On tham sûthportice ;   sêo sâwul is mid Christe.

As soon as he landed,   on the ship they him blinded,
And him thus blind   brought (they) to the monks
And there he dwelt   (all) the while he lived.
Afterwards they him buried,   as him well befitted,
At the west end,   the steeple (tower) hard by,
In the south portal ;   his soul is with Christ.

Rimes like lende: blende, wunode: lufode, byrigde:
gebyrde, ende: gehénde, porticé: Christé, are unmistakable, and the two halves of each line make a couplet.

It is important to note these symptoms. They show
how erroneous it would be to attribute the disintegra-
tion of the early language and literature solely to the
Norman Conquest. The truth is that tendencies to
change had long been at work in England, no less
than in Germany. Thus there are several riming passages in Cynewulf's poems and in the *Phoenix.* But
the English maintained their primitive system longer
than the Germans, for the victory of rime over allit-

eration was complete in Germany by the end of the
9th century. Even had the Normans never invaded
England, the English would have developed eight and
ten-syllable riming couplets in imitation of the French,
just as the Germans did. And they would also have
patterned their literature after the French romances
that were then fast becoming the fashion. The Norman Conquest accelerated the substitution of rime for
alliteration, and the importation of romance-literature.
But the process would have gone on, more slowly, it
is true, without the Normans.

In evidence that literary taste in England was changing, it will suffice to cite the fact that the story of
Apollonius of Tyre and the *Letters of Alexander the
Great to Aristotle,* fabulous subjects taken from the
later Greek prose romances, were translated into English
before the Conquest. The Old-German heroic spirit
and heroic verse were doomed to pass away before the
new era of sentimentality and adventure.

www.ingramcontent.com/pod-product-compliance
Lightning Source LLC
Chambersburg PA
CBHW020242090426
42735CB00010B/1807